THAILAND

Punprapar Klinchui

OCTOPUS BOOKS

Acknowledgments

Editor: Diana Craig
Art Editor: David Rowley
Designer: Sue Storey
Copy Editor: Jenni Fleetwood
Production Controller: Trevor Jones

Special Photography: James Murphy
Food Preparation: Dolly Meers
Styling: Sarah Wiley
Illustrations: David Sim

The publishers wish to thank the following for providing photographs for this book: Tore Gill/ Ace Photo Agency page 5; The Hutchison Library page 7

Title page: Steamed Curry in Artichoke Cups (page 34)

All recipes are for 4 servings unless otherwise stated

First published in 1987 by
Octopus Books Limited
59 Grosvenor Street
London W1X 9DA

ISBN 0 7064 3097 2

Printed in Hong Kong

Contents

THAILAND

W hen you turn the pages of this book you will quickly become aware of the 'uniqueness' of Thai cooking, and once you have sampled some of Punprapar Klinchui's recipes, you will understand why this is so. From the tasty snacks that the Thai people nibble throughout the day to the main-meal hot and spicy soups, fiery curries, and crisp, crunchy and colourful side salads, you will quickly discover the many different delights of this cuisine.

Thai food appeals to more than taste alone, for to the Thai cook a dish should appeal equally well to the eye and nose as well as the palate. Even for the simplest of meals, great attention is paid to detail, both to the appearance and presentation of each dish and to the subtleties and nuances of aromas and flavours. Thai cooking is not an exact science; 'recipes' have been handed down by word of mouth from one generation of cooks to another (the first known recipes in print did not appear until after the First World War), and each cook has added his or her own individual touch. Although exact quantities are given for each recipe in this book, no Thai cook would adhere to these rigidly. If you are trying Thai food for the first time, don't be daunted by the exquisite marrying of flavours, nor by the meticulous presentation. Just a little effort guarantees beautiful and delicious results.

Right: The palm-fringed coast of Thailand

5

History and Background

The uniqueness of Thai cuisine stems from one simple fact: Thailand is the only South-East Asian country never to have been colonised, never to have been subject to foreign rule. If Thai cuisine bears any resemblance to other cuisines it is only to those of its neighbours China, Burma and India. Indeed, the Thai people originally came from southern China, but were driven out by the Mongols and finally settled between Burma to the north-west and Malaysia to the south. By the end of the eighteenth century the Thais had established a permanent capital city in the heart of the Chao Pra Ya river basin — the site of present-day Bangkok. The new country was then known as Siam.

The Siamese kings quickly became noted for their devotion to good living and most notably to good food, and the palace kitchens were amply provided for by this new, rich and fertile land. From the mountainous north came meat, game and freshwater fish. The more fertile south provided an absolute abundance of tropical fruits and vegetables, seafood from the Gulf of Siam and fragrant rice from the Chao Pra Ya basin. Spices and other exotica came to the Siamese ports by way of merchant traders from India and the Middle East.

One of the best ways to capture the flavour of Thai cuisine is to see the canals of modern-day Bangkok with the famous 'floating market'. Sampans loaded with dew-fresh fruits and vegetables of the highest quality indicate how the tradition of good food has been passed on to the modern Thais, rich and poor alike. In fact everywhere you go in Bangkok you will be struck by the enormous variety of different foods on display, from the fresh produce of the floating market to the rice barges and fishing boats, noodle and porridge (*khow tom*) stalls on virtually every street corner, the number of floating restaurants and barges, trolleys and motor-cycles selling and delivering every imaginable kind of food.

Customs and Menus

The giving and sharing of food are an essential part of Thai culture. Buddhism is still a strong faith in Thailand today, and at some time in his life every Thai male should become a monk — for at least three months, when he will have to beg for his food every day around the local neighbourhood.

The sharing of food is extended to the family table. Food is always placed in serving bowls in the centre of the table so that everyone can help themselves. The custom of giving each person an individual serving as in the majority of Western countries is unknown in Thailand. Instead everyone serves themselves from communal bowls. Sharing food is also a sign of great hospitality. A Thai family considers it a great honour to share their meal with a visitor, no matter how humble the meal may be.

In the country districts throughout Thailand, the way of life has not changed greatly over the years (though in Bangkok and other large cities Western influences have gradually crept in). In rural districts, a typical day starts at around five in the morning with a visit to the local market to buy the day's fresh produce. Breakfast is one of the largest meals of the day for most Thais. Rice or porridge is always served, plus a curried dish (*kang*) of some sort, fried vegetables, fish or meat, and maybe an omelette.

Lunch is a lighter, plainer meal than breakfast, and usually consists of a noodle dish with meat, fish and vegetables. City dwellers buy their noodles from the numerous special noodle cafés and restaurants or from street noodle vendors — there are noodle kiosks and floating barges at every turn in Bangkok. Even in the country noodle vendors push their wares round from house to house on trolleys.

'Snacks' are hugely popular throughout the day, but particularly in the afternoon. They include *satay*, bite-sized spring rolls, *geow grob* (fried wonton) and crispy rice dishes.

The evening meal is the highspot of the day in virtually every Thai home. Traditionally this meal consists of at least five dishes, all of which are served at the same time. In Thai restaurants in the West food is often served in separate courses to cater to the Western style of eating, but this is not authentic. For example, starters are not traditionally served at the beginning of a Thai meal, although in a Thai restaurant you will often find that 'snacks' such as spring rolls, *satay* and wonton are served as starters, and soups are listed as a separate course. In an authentic Thai meal, soup is always served at the same time as the other dishes and is drunk with a spoon from individual bowls throughout the meal.

The purpose of serving at least five dishes is to ensure a well-balanced, harmonious meal, an important factor when all the different dishes are served at the same time. Plain rice, the staple food of the Thais, is the central dish, accompanied by a hot curried dish (*kang*) of meat, poultry or fish in a sauce or gravy, a quick stir-fried dish (*bhud*), a crisp salad (*yam*), a soup (*tom yum*) and a spicy hot dipping sauce called *nam prig* which is on the table at just about every Thai meal. Sometimes a whole baked or steamed fish is also served. One thing is certain, the cook will consider carefully the balance of the different dishes, which will complement each other in colour, aroma, texture and flavour.

There are many Thai desserts, most of which are based on custard mixtures and coconut milk and are very sweet. These are not generally served after an everyday meal, but reserved for special occasions such as formal banquets and wedding parties or eaten as a snack during the day with sweetmeats and sweet cakes which are bought ready-made. Seasonal fresh fruit is normally eaten after a meal to refresh the palate — pomelos, mangoes, pawpaws, melons, pineapples, plums and 'rose' apples are widely grown. As with most Thai food the fruit is generally beautifully presented — fruit 'carving' is an art which many Thai girls learn from an early age, carving intricate shapes of flowers, birds and butterflies out of fruit and vegetables. Petals and flower heads are often used for garnishing and decorating.

How to Eat Thai Food

Each diner has his or her own dinner plate set in front of them, together with a spoon and fork and a soup bowl. Chopsticks are seldom used in Thailand. Food is cut into small pieces so it can be served and eaten easily — knives are not used at the table. The diners first help themselves to a spoonful or two of rice, then a spoonful of one of the other dishes is placed on each plate next to the rice. After this has been eaten, another spoonful of rice is taken and a small portion of another dish. This

6

A market stall in Bangkok

process is then repeated until the meal is finished. Thai people always eat one dish at a time in this way; each dish has been so carefully composed that its flavour would be spoilt if mixed with others. Each dish must be savoured in its own right, with a spoonful of plain rice *next* to it, to act as a foil. It is well worth remembering this when eating in a Thai restaurant. Never pile rice on your plate and spoon curry or a stir-fried dish over it. Fried rice is considered a meal in its own right to Thai people and is eaten for lunch or as a mid-afternoon or even late supper snack. Plain boiled or steamed rice is the only rice which is eaten as part of a main meal.

Combining Tastes & Textures

Because all Thai dishes are served together, no one dish is considered more important than another. The accent is on balance of flavour, texture and colour, and exquisite flavours are achieved by the careful blending of many different ingredients. The flavours of Thai food are hot and spicy, sweet, sour and salty. This combination comes from the use of a number of different ingredients which are used over and over again in Thai food. Garlic, fresh root ginger and many different kinds of chillies (some of them searingly hot) are frequently used; so too are fresh coconut and coconut milk, galanga (*khar*), lemon grass (*takrai*), citrus rind and citrus leaves, the fresh green leaves of mint and basil and the root, stem and leaves of coriander. The combination of these ingredients, with the Thai fish gravy known as nam pla, dried shrimps and dried shrimp paste (*kapee*) also make the flavour of Thai food quite unique; so too does the use of sugar in many savoury dishes.

Thai curries are very different from their Indian counterparts in that they are not made with dried spices but with a fresh, wet spice paste made from ginger, garlic, chillies, lemon grass, fresh coriander, dried shrimp paste and galanga. Coconut milk and cream are

also frequently included in Thai curries. The milk is used to cook the meat at the beginning, then the coconut cream is added with the wet curry paste, until the oil separates. Most Thai cooks pound the fresh ingredients for the curry paste each day using a mortar and pestle, although it can be bought freshly made at the market. There are three main types of Thai curry: the sour *kang som,* the hot red *kang bhed* based on red chillies and chilli powder, and the green *kang keaw whan,* which is made with tiny green chillies and is fiery hot. Thai food has a reputation for being fiery hot and even the salads often have tiny green chillies hidden amongst their leafy ingredients, but the hotness of Thai food largely depends on the individual cook and the majority of Thai dishes are not too hot at all. Those who like their food fiery hot add more *nam prig* at the table.

Preparation and Equipment

Like Chinese food, Thai food takes quite a long time to prepare, but as the cooking time is so short, great advantage can be gained in preparing everything in advance, then quickly assembling the dish at the end — this is especially useful when entertaining. Ingredients are very finely sliced on the diagonal or neatly chopped, then set out before cooking so that one by one they can be whisked into the pan. Apart from knives, there are very few other pieces of equipment necessary. Most Thai cooks use a cleaver to chop large pieces of meat and whole birds into bite-sized pieces, but this can be done with a sharp knife. Most Thai meals are cooked over a charcoal stove, although gas and electric cookers are common in urban areas now. A Chinese-style wok for Thai stir-fry dishes, and a steamer for fish, vege-tables and rice are good ideas. A special kind of granite mortar and pestle is used for pounding wet spice pastes; these are difficult to obtain in the West, but a porcelain equivalent can be used, or a food processor.

Special Ingredients

Bamboo shoots: Widely available in cans, sliced or unsliced, these are the tender young shoots of the bamboo plant which are harvested in winter and parboiled. Creamy in colour, they are most often used in Thai stir-fried dishes. After opening, store them in cold water and change twice daily; they can then be kept for up to 7 days.

Bean curd: This is available fresh at health food shops and some supermarkets as well as oriental stores. For Thai recipes choose the firm bean curd rather than the soft 'silken' Japanese variety called *tofu*. Bean curd is made from puréed soya beans and is highly nutritious — rich in protein yet low in fat. It is white in colour with a soft cheesy texture, and can be sliced or cubed. Its bland flavour makes it a good recipient for the pungent ingredients which are so often used in Thai cooking. If stored in the refrigerator, fresh bean curd will keep for several days; vacuum-packed 'long-life' bean curd is also available and this can keep for several months.

Chillies: Used frequently in Thai recipes, the favourite variety are the tiny green chillies called *prig khee nhoo*. These are fiery hot and should be treated with caution.

Chilli sauce: This commercially prepared bottled sauce is used for its fiery effect in many savoury dishes. It is a mixture of hot, sweet and salty flavours and is generally used in small quantities.

Eggplants: The variety used in Thai cooking are small and green and should not be confused with the larger purple aubergines which are also known as eggplants from their American name. Small green eggplants are often eaten raw in salads in Thailand, and are highly prized for their crunchy texture — they are very pippy inside.

Fish sauce (nam pla): This commercially prepared bottled sauce is made from salted anchovies, and is very thin in consistency but strong in flavour. It is widely used in Thai cooking to accentuate the flavours of other ingredients, rather than impart its own 'fishy' flavour. There are many different brands, varying in colour from pale to dark brown, and some stronger and saltier than others, so it is worth trying several to find the one you like best.

Galanga (khar): A member of the ginger family, galanga is a root with an earthy, pine-like fragrance. It is prepared like fresh ginger, but as it is woodier it is more difficult to peel and crush. Conveniently, it is also available in powdered form under the name *laos*, and 1 teaspoon *laos* powder is equivalent to about 1 cm/½ inch of the root.

Ginger (khing): This is used in its fresh form in Thai cooking. It is a rhizome with a thick skin which should be peeled, then finely chopped or crushed before cooking, according to individual recipe requirements. Fresh root

ginger is widely available; ground ginger powder should not be used as a substitute in Thai cooking.

Glutinous rice: Also called 'sticky' rice, this is a short-grain rice which sticks together when cooked. In North-Eastern Thailand, it is eaten as a main dish, but in Bangkok and other cities it is only used in the making of desserts. The variety of rice eaten with meals is long-grain fragrant Thai rice.

Gui chai leaves: These leaves look like a grassy version of spring onions but have a more distinctive flavour. They are often chopped and added to fried noodle dishes. Gui chai leaves are sold fresh in oriental stores;

1) Pineapple; 2) Theoy leaves; 3) Lime; 4) Baby corn cobs; 5) Chilli peppers; 6) Lychees; 7) Lemon; 8) Taro root; 9) Rice vermicelli; 10) Jelly mushrooms; 11) Ginger root; 12) Krachai root; 13) Peeled water chestnuts; 14) Bamboo shoots; 15) Palm sugar; 16) Agar agar (seaweed jelly); 17) Whole peanuts; 18) Lotus seeds; 19) Green peppercorns; 20) Bean curd; 21) Eggplants; 22) Chilli powder; 23) Thai chillies; 24) Wonton wrappers

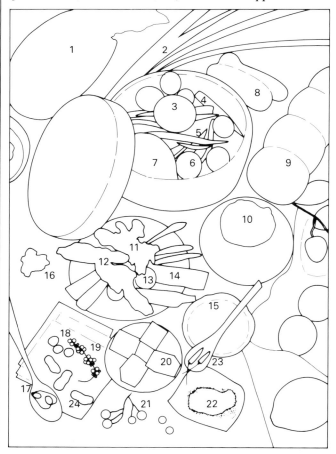

if unobtainable, spring onions can be used as a substitute, but the flavour of the finished dish will be milder.

Jelly mushrooms (hed hunu): A variety of fungus, jelly mushrooms are also called 'cloud ears' because their appearance resembles an ear. They are sold dried and must be soaked in water before use when they will swell up and look gelatinous. They are liked for their crunchy texture rather than their flavour, which is somewhat bland.

Krachai root: This tuber has a strong, distinctive aroma, and is available fresh and dried: fresh krachai is preferable to dried, however. It is one of the main ingredients in Thai curry pastes, and in most fish curries. To prepare krachai, simply scrape off the fine brown skin with a sharp knife, then chop the flesh finely.

Lemon grass (takrai): A highly aromatic plant with a very strong lemon fragrance and flavour. The bulbous root end is sliced, chopped or crushed like fresh root ginger, whereas the stem end is added whole to curries and soups and removed before serving. Lemon grass is widely available fresh, although the dried powder known as *serai* can be used instead. If substituting dried for fresh, 1 teaspoon *serai* is equivalent to 1 stem of lemon grass.

Lotus seeds (med bua): Available in cans, these are the seeds of the lotus flower. They are used in many Thai desserts and puddings. The Chinese also use them for sweet dishes and they are easy to obtain at any Chinese shop.

Maggi sauce: This liquid seasoning is used extensively in Thailand, both as an ingredient in cooking and as a table condiment. It is a thin brown sauce available in bottles from supermarkets.

Makrut: The peel and leaves of this rather ugly-looking citrus fruit are used, for their strong flavour, in curry pastes and soups. If unavailable, lime, grapefruit or lemon can be used instead.

Matsaman curry paste: This is available in jars and is well worth buying to make the famous Indian-style Matsaman curry. The paste is made from such a large number of different ingredients that it would take a long time to prepare at home.

Oyster sauce: A commercially prepared bottled sauce, made from oysters and soy sauce. Thick, brown and strongly flavoured, it is used frequently in Thai cooking to add extra flavour to meat, fish, poultry and vegetable dishes, particularly stir-fries.

Palm sugar: Obtained from the sap of coconut, Nippah and Plamyrah palms, this sticky and strongly flavoured sugar is sold in the form of flat cakes. Unrefined dark brown barbados sugar can be used instead.

Pickled fish (pla rah): Various types of fish are pickled – the most common being anchovies, but other small fish are also used. Sold in jars, *pla rah* is the strongest condiment used in Thai cooking and you can be sure that any dish in which it is included will have pronounced salty and fishy flavours.

Pickled garlic: Thai garlic is small and the bulbs are pickled whole, in a sweet and sour brine, and sold in jars. Garlic pickled in the Middle East tends to be larger and is therefore more often pickled in separate cloves. Either can be used in Thai recipes.

Pickled turnips: These are soaked in salted water then dried, and so are very salty. They are sold in packets. For dishes that require extra saltiness they can be used straight from the packet and finely chopped, but if they are required to be less salty they are washed in water before use and the saltiness squeezed out. Pickled radishes are also available, and the two can be used interchangeably in recipes.

Salted soya beans (tao chiew): These have a very special flavour and are added by the spoonful according to taste – they go exceptionally well in any dish containing ginger. They are used as a flavouring ingredient in many savoury dishes, particularly stir-fries, and are sold in jars.

Seaweed jelly: A natural setting agent made from seaweed and used in the making of desserts. It can be bought at health food shops and oriental stores in long white strands or powder form, under the name *agar-agar*. Agar-agar is colourless and tasteless and, when used in very small quantities, can set a large volume of liquid. Gelatine can be used as a substitute; 4 tablespoons gelatine is equivalent to 25 g (1 oz) agar-agar.

Soy sauce: Made from fermented soya beans, soy sauce comes in two varieties – light and dark. Light soy sauce is light in colour as its name suggests, but is quite salty in flavour. It is used in Thai cooking instead of fish sauce whenever a fishy flavour is not required, such as in chicken or stir-fried rice dishes. Dark soy sauce is dark in colour but it is also thicker and sweeter than light soy sauce, and is not so salty. It is most frequently used in noodle dishes.

Tamarind: This is the fruit of a tropical tree and is used for its acidic flavour. The individual fruits resemble bean pods. They are sold dried or pulped and must be soaked in warm water for 5 to 10 minutes before use. After cooking, the tamarind is then squeezed to extract as much pulp as possible, and the pulp and soaking water is then sieved and used in cooking. Tamarind has a very strong flavour, and only a walnut-sized piece should be used; the longer the soaking time, the stronger-flavoured the liquid will be.

Taro root: This vegetable is similar to a sweet potato and is available in West Indian shops as well as oriental stores. Thai cooks boil it or steam it and serve it as a vegetable; it is also used in some puddings.

Theoy leaves: Also known as *pandanus*, these are the long and narrow green leaves of the *pandanus latifolia* plant. They are used as a flavouring and colouring in savoury and sweet dishes. There is no substitute for their flavour, which is quite distinctive, but sometimes green food colouring is used as a substitute for the colour, especially in sweets.

Vermicelli: A very common ingredient in Thai cooking. Two main types of dried vermicelli are used. *Sen mee* are dried noodles made from rice flour, often called 'rice sticks' because they are so very fine. They can be deep-fried straight from the packet or soaked in water and boiled, according to the dish in which they are being used. The second main variety, *wun sen*, are transparent or cellophane noodles made from mung bean flour. They are very fine dried noodles which need to be soaked in water before use.

Water chestnuts: These are used for their crisp and crunchy texture rather than their flavour, which is rather bland. Fresh water chestnuts are sometimes available at specialist shops, and their brownish-black skin must be peeled off with a sharp knife to reveal the white walnut-sized bulb inside. Canned water chestnuts are ready-peeled; they are widely available and inexpensive.

Wonton wrappers: These wrappers or skins are small squares of wafer-thin noodle dough made from flour, egg and water. Available fresh and frozen at oriental stores, they are filled with savoury mixtures, then boiled, steamed or deep-fried.

Menus

Menu 1

Hot and Sour Prawn Soup
Prawns with Curry Topping
Chicken with Baby Corn Cobs
Fried Red Curry with Pork and Beans
Fried Eggs with Pork Sauce

Menu 2

Clear Bean Curd Soup
Fish in Garlic Sauce
Sweet and Sour Pork
Thick Red Beef Curry
Prawn Salad with Lemon Grass

Menu 3

Fish with Tamarind Juice and Ginger
Seafood in Batter
Fried Beef with Chilli and Bamboo Shoots
(see variation, Pork with Chilli and Basil)
Red Pork Curry
Shrimp Dipping Sauce

Menu 4

Clear Tapioca Soup
Fish in Tamarind Sauce
Green Chicken Curry

(see variation, Red Pork Curry, and use green curry paste (page 63))
Beef with Mushrooms and Oyster Sauce
Shrimp Paste Sauce

Menu 5

Chicken and Coconut Soup
Crab in the Shell
Beef with Ginger and Jelly Mushrooms
Sour Fish Curry
Hard-Boiled Eggs with Tamarind Sauce

Menu 6

Clear Vermicelli Soup
Fish with Ginger and Soya Flavouring
Steamed Curry in Artichoke Cups
Chicken in Theoy Leaves
Beef and Bamboo Shoot Salad

Menu 7
Barbecue Party

Pork Fillet on Skewers
Grilled Fish
Stuffed Chicken Wings
Grilled Chicken Sala Thai Style
Pork Spare Ribs

11

Snacks & Soups

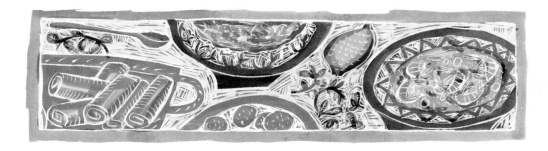

Thai people love their food and are prepared to take great trouble over it even if it is only a snack to nibble between meals. Thai snacks do require a little skill and practice to prepare, but they are so delicious that they are well worth the effort. Thai snacks should, correctly, be eaten on their own, but they can be served as starters in the Western manner.

Thai soups should never be starters, but should be served along with the main meal. Unlike puréed Western soups, Thai soups are a balanced combination of different ingredients which are left whole and which retain their individual taste and texture.

12

Fried Bread Shapes

Kah Nom Pung Nah Mhoo

75 g (3 oz) raw prawns (see page 63)
100 g (4 oz) minced pork
1 tablespoon finely chopped fresh coriander leaves
1 tablespoon finely chopped spring onion or onion
1 teaspoon garlic mixture (see page 62)
1 tablespoon nam pla (fish gravy)
1 egg, beaten
5 slices white bread
plum sauce, to serve (see page 62)

Finely chop the prawns in a food processor or blender, or by hand on a wooden board. Transfer the prawns to a bowl and add the minced pork, coriander leaves, spring onion, garlic mixture and nam pla. Mix the egg in well.

Cut each slice of bread into 6 pieces of more or less equal size, using decorative cutters if liked.

Spread each piece of bread with a little of the pork and prawn mixture, using a knife to press the mixture firmly on to the bread.

Heat oil to a depth of about 2.5 cm (1 inch) in a large frying pan and add the pieces of bread, a few at a time, with the topping side downwards. Cook over moderate heat for 6 to 8 minutes, then turn over and cook the other side of the bread until golden.

Drain on paper towels and serve hot with plum sauce, if liked.

Variation: The prawns may be omitted from the recipe and the quantity of pork doubled, if preferred. Serve this variation with Cucumber Salad (see page 53) or chilli sauce. Alternatively, make the topping mixture with flaked crab meat or a mixture of crab and pork.

Fried Wonton

Geow Grob

225 g (8 oz) minced pork
1 tablespoon finely chopped onion
2 teaspoons garlic mixture (see page 62)
½ tablespoon nam pla (fish gravy)
20 wonton wrappers (see Note)
1 egg yolk
oil for deep-frying

Combine the minced pork, onion, garlic mixture and nam pla in a bowl. Stir well.

Place 1 teaspoon of the mixture in the centre of a wonton wrapper. Fold the wrapper to enclose the filling in a neat triangle, sealing the edges with egg yolk. Fill the remaining wonton wrappers in the same way.

Heat the oil in a wok or deep-fat fryer and deep-fry

Pork Fillet on Skewers (Satay) with peanut sauce, cucumber salad and toast

the filled wonton, a few at a time, for about 5 minutes or until golden brown. Drain on paper towels.

Serve hot, with a selection of sauces, such as plum sauce (see page 62), sweet and sour or chilli sauce. **Note:** Wonton wrappers are sold ready-made in some Oriental supermarkets. A 500 g (1 lb) package will hold about 90 wrappers. If tightly wrapped in cling film, the wrappers will keep for up to 1 week in the refrigerator.

Pork Fillet on Skewers

Satay

500 g (1 lb) pork fillet
1 teaspoon salt
2 teaspoons palm sugar or brown sugar
1 teaspoon ground turmeric
1 teaspoon ground coriander
1 teaspoon ground cumin
175 ml (6 fl oz) coconut milk

Peanut sauce:
50 g (2 oz) roasted peanuts
1 teaspoon salt
300 ml (10 fl oz) coconut milk
2 teaspoons red curry paste (see page 63)
2 tablespoons sugar
½ teaspoon tamarind juice (see page 62) or lemon juice

Cut the pork into 5 cm (2 inch) long strips and place in a large bowl. Add the salt, sugar, turmeric, coriander, cumin and 4 tablespoons of the coconut milk.

Mix thoroughly, using clean hands to knead the spices into the meat. Cover and set aside to marinate for at least 2 hours.

Meanwhile make the sauce. Grind the peanuts with the salt in a mortar until the mixture has the consistency of thick cream. Set aside.

Place half the coconut milk in a saucepan with the curry paste. Heat gently, stirring constantly, for 3 minutes. Stir in the creamed peanuts with the sugar, tamarind juice and remaining coconut milk.

Simmer over gentle heat for 20 to 30 minutes, stirring occasionally to prevent the mixture sticking to the bottom of the pan. Transfer to a bowl.

Thread the pork strips on to oiled bamboo skewers: this quantity of meat should fill 16 to 20 skewers. Grill on a barbecue over medium hot coals, or under a grill, for 12 to 15 minutes until cooked through, turning several times and brushing with the remaining coconut milk frequently during cooking.

Serve with peanut sauce, a salad of cucumber and onion (see page 53) and triangles of white toast, if liked. **Variation:** Fillet steak or breast of chicken may be used instead of pork fillet.

14

Above: Spring Rolls; below: Pork on Pineapple

Thai Dumplings

Kah Nom Jeeb

225 g (8 oz) finely minced pork
225 g (8 oz) crab meat or raw prawns, shelled,
deveined and finely chopped (see page 63)
1 egg
100 g (4 oz) canned water chestnuts, drained
1 tablespoon garlic mixture (see page 62)
1 tablespoon nam pla (fish gravy)
1 tablespoon soy sauce
1 tablespoon cornflour
40 wonton wrappers
20 raw prawns, shelled, deveined and cut in half
lengthways
oil for deep-frying

To serve:
4 tablespoons soy sauce
4 tablespoons sweet and sour sauce
1 tablespoon garlic oil (see page 63)

Combine the first 8 ingredients in a food processor with a steel blade and process until well mixed but not puréed. Alternatively knead the ingredients by hand.

Trim 1 cm (½ inch) off the 4 corners of each wonton wrapper to make an octagonal shape. Place a generous teaspoon of the mixture in the centre of each wonton wrapper and bring up the edges all round to form a cup shape. Pinch the sides of the wonton 'cup' between forefinger and thumb to form pleats. Tuck half a prawn into each wonton dumpling.

Arrange the filled dumplings in the top of one or two greased steamers, and steam for 15 minutes.

Prepare the dipping sauce by mixing the soy sauce and sweet and sour sauce in a small bowl. Serve with the hot dumplings, sprinkled with garlic oil.

Spring Rolls

Poh Piah Tod

1 × 225 g (8 oz) package spring roll wrappers, each
wrapper approximately 13 cm (5 inches) square

Filling:
100 g (4 oz) jelly mushrooms (soaked weight)
2 tablespoons vegetable oil
2 tablespoons garlic mixture (see page 62)
100 g (4 oz) crab meat
100 g (4 oz) raw prawns, shelled, deveined and finely
chopped (see page 63)
100 g (4 oz) minced pork
100 g (4 oz) vermicelli, soaked in boiling water until
soft and then cut in 1 cm (½ inch) lengths
2 tablespoons nam pla (fish gravy)
2 tablespoons light soy sauce
1 teaspoon sugar
5 spring onions or 1 medium onion, finely chopped
1 egg, beaten
oil for deep-frying

First make the filling. Soak the jelly mushrooms in boiling water for 20 minutes. Drain, squeezing out excess liquid, remove stems and chop finely.

Heat the vegetable oil in a wok or large frying pan. Add the garlic mixture and stir-fry for 1 minute. Add the crab meat, chopped prawns and minced pork and stir-fry for 10 to 12 minutes or until lightly cooked. Add the vermicelli, mushrooms, nam pla, soy sauce, sugar and chopped onion, and cook for 5 minutes, stirring constantly, until all the liquid has been absorbed. Remove the pan from the heat and set aside until cool.

Meanwhile, carefully separate the spring roll wrappers, spreading them on a clean tea towel, and keeping them covered with a second towel or with cling film (exposure to the air will cause them to harden). Place about 2 tablespoons of the filling on the lower half of one of the spring roll wrappers. Brush the left and right borders with beaten egg. Fold the bottom edge up, bring the left and right sides over the filling, and roll the wrapper up like a sausage. Brush the top edge with more beaten egg and seal. Make the remaining spring rolls in the same way, keeping the filled rolls covered.

Heat the oil in a wok or deep-fat fryer and cook the spring rolls, a few at a time, for 5 to 8 minutes or until golden brown. Drain on paper towels, and serve hot with sweet and sour sauce and a mixed salad with pineapple cubes, if liked.

Pork on Pineapple

Mah Hoh

3½ tablespoons vegetable oil
½ tablespoon chopped dried red chilli
1 tablespoon garlic mixture (see page 62)
100 g (4 oz) minced pork
100 g (4 oz) raw prawns, shelled, deveined and finely
chopped (see page 63)
2 tablespoons nam pla (fish gravy)
2 tablespoons brown sugar
50 g (2 oz) peanuts, finely ground
1 large pineapple
fresh coriander leaves, to garnish

In a small frying pan, heat ½ tablespoon of the oil and fry the dried red chilli until crisp. Drain on paper towels.

Heat the remaining oil in a medium saucepan, add the garlic mixture and stir-fry for 2 minutes. Add the pork and prawns and cook for 5 to 6 minutes, stirring frequently to break up any lumps. Stir in the nam pla and sugar and cook for a further 10 to 15 minutes, stirring, until the mixture is thick and sticky.

Add the ground peanuts, stir well, and remove the pan from the heat.

Peel and core the pineapple and cut the flesh into 5 cm (2 inch) squares. Arrange the squares on a large serving platter and top each with 1 teaspoon of the pork mixture. Garnish with coriander leaves and chilli.

Variation: This dish is equally effective if oranges are used instead of pineapple. Peel and segment 6 oranges. Using a sharp knife, split each orange segment down the fleshy curve and open it out like a small pocket. Top with the pork mixture.

Chicken Dumplings

Kha Nom Jeeb Sai Gai

3 tablespoons glutinous rice flour
250 g (9 oz) rice flour plus 2 tablespoons
3 tablespoons arrowroot
350 ml (12 fl oz) water
2½ tablespoons vegetable oil
banana leaves for steaming (see Note)

Filling:
4 tablespoons vegetable oil
2 tablespoons garlic mixture (see page 62)
450 g (1 lb) minced chicken
1 medium onion, finely chopped
3 tablespoons nam pla (fish gravy)
3 tablespoons sugar

To serve:
1–2 tablespoons garlic oil (see page 63)
1 lettuce, separated into leaves
½ cucumber, sliced
1 bunch spring onions, sliced
French dressing (optional)

First prepare the dough. Place the glutinous rice flour in a heavy bottomed saucepan with 250 g (9 oz) of the rice flour and 1 tablespoon of the arrowroot. Stir in the water and oil.

Place the pan over moderate heat and cook, stirring constantly, until the mixture forms a ball, leaving the sides of the pan clean.

Transfer the mixture to a bowl and allow to cool slightly. When the dough is just warm, add the remaining rice flour and arrowroot and knead until smooth and shiny. Cover the bowl with a damp cloth and set aside while preparing the filling.

Heat 2 tablespoons of the oil in a frying pan, add the garlic mixture and stir-fry for 1 minute. Add the chicken and stir-fry for 3 to 5 minutes or until cooked. Stir in the onion, nam pla and sugar and cook, stirring, until all the liquid has been absorbed. Spoon the mixture into a bowl and set aside until cold.

Roll the dough into small balls, about 1 cm (½ inch) in diameter, then flatten each ball to a round. Place about 1 heaped teaspoon of filling in the centre of each round. Draw up the sides to enclose the filling in an onion shape. Alternatively, place the filling on one half of each dough round, and fold the remaining halves over to form semi-circles. Crimp the edges, pasty-fashion.

Place a layer of torn banana leaves in the top of a steamer. Brush the leaves generously with the remaining oil and prick them all over with a fork.

Arrange the dumplings on top of the banana leaves. Place over boiling water and steam for 10 to 15 minutes until cooked.

To serve, brush the dumplings generously with garlic oil and arrange on a large platter. Serve with a lettuce, cucumber and spring onion salad.

Note: If banana leaves are not available for steaming, foil may be used instead.

16

Egg Nests with Pork and Prawn Filling

Lhrum

6 eggs, lightly beaten
2 red chillies, seeded and cut into short thin strips
4 tablespoons fresh coriander leaves

Filling:
3 tablespoons vegetable oil
1 tablespoon garlic mixture (see page 62)
225 g (8 oz) minced pork
100 g (4 oz) shelled prawns, minced
2 tablespoons finely chopped onion
3 tablespoons nam pla (fish gravy)
3 tablespoons sugar
100 g (4 oz) roasted peanuts, crushed

In Thailand, the egg nests are traditionally made by dipping clean fingertips in beaten egg and spattering the surface of an oiled frying pan in the required shape. This takes practice, however, so a simpler method, using a piping bag, is suggested below.

Prepare the filling. Heat 2 tablespoons of the oil in a wok or frying pan, add the garlic mixture and stir-fry for 1 minute. Add the pork and stir-fry for 5 to 7 minutes, then add all the remaining ingredients except the peanuts and cook, stirring, for 3 minutes.

Remove the pan from the heat, add the peanuts and set aside.

Brush a large clean frying pan with some of the remaining oil. Place the pan over moderate heat. Fit a 5 mm (¼ inch) tube into a piping bag. Spoon a little of the beaten egg mixture into the bag, keeping the nozzle stopped with a finger. Hold the bag over the frying pan, remove the fingertip and drizzle the egg into the centre of the pan to form a lattice shape, about 9 cm (3½ inches) square.

As soon as the egg lattice is cooked, slide it on to a plate and keep warm. Continue to make lattices until all the egg mixture has been used, brushing the frying pan with more oil as necessary.

To make the nests, make a cross from 2 pieces of chilli in the centre of each egg lattice square. Place a coriander leaf on top of the chilli and add 1 heaped teaspoon of the prepared filling.

Carefully fold the egg lattice over the filling to form parcel shapes and arrange these on a serving platter so that the red of the chilli and the green of the coriander can clearly be seen. Serve immediately.

Left: Deep-Fried Corn Cakes; right: Chicken Dumplings

Deep-Fried Corn Cakes

Tod Mun Khow Phode

450 g (1 lb) fresh corn on the cob
450 g (1 lb) minced pork (not too lean)
1 tablespoon garlic mixture (see page 62)
1–2 eggs, beaten
2 tablespoons plain flour
1 tablespoon cornflour
1 teaspoon salt
2 tablespoons light soy sauce
oil for deep frying
½ cube vegetable stock, crumbled (optional)

To serve:
1 large cucumber, sliced
2 chillies, cut into thin rings
2 tablespoons fresh coriander leaves

This is a popular Thai snack, often served at cocktail parties.

Working over a mixing bowl, slice all the kernels from the corn cobs with a sharp knife. Add the pork and garlic mixture and mix well, then stir in one of the beaten eggs.

Add the flours, salt and soy sauce, stirring thoroughly to make a mixture capable of being shaped. If necessary add part or all of the second egg.

Break off a small piece of the mixture and test fry in a little of the oil. If too bland, add the half cube of vegetable stock, working it into the mixture.

Form the mixture into flat round cakes, about 4 cm (1½ inches) in diameter.

Heat the remaining oil in a deep-fat fryer or wok and deep-fry the cakes, a few at a time, until golden. Drain on paper towels, and allow to cool.

To serve, place each corn cake on a cucumber ring and top with a chilli ring and a coriander leaf. Secure with a cocktail stick.

Arrange the corn cakes on a serving platter, surrounded by any remaining cucumber slices.

Pork Spare Ribs

Seeh Krong Mhoo

500 g (1 lb) pork spare ribs
2 tablespoons garlic mixture (see page 62)
1 teaspoon salt
2 tablespoons dark soy sauce
1 teaspoon ground ginger
1 tablespoon brown sugar
2 tablespoons honey

Cut the spare ribs into individual portions.

Mix all the remaining ingredients in a shallow heatproof dish large enough to hold all the ribs in a single layer. Add the ribs, stir well to coat them with the mixture, cover and set aside for at least 2 hours.

Remove the cover and bake the spare ribs in a preheated moderate oven, 180°C (350°F), Gas Mark 4 for 1½ hours.

To finish the dish, grill the ribs on a barbecue over medium hot coals for 20 to 30 minutes, or under a preheated grill.

Serve hot, accompanied by a green salad.

Tapioca Balls

Sakoo Sord Sai

500 g (1 lb) tapioca
1 litre (1¾ pints) hot water
25 g (1 oz) finely chopped dried pickled turnip
3 tablespoons vegetable oil
3 tablespoons garlic mixture (see page 62)
225 g (8 oz) chicken breast, minced or very finely chopped
100 g (4 oz) onion, finely chopped
4 tablespoons nam pla (fish gravy)
75 g (3 oz) brown sugar

To garnish:
1 small lettuce, separated into leaves
6 spring onions, trimmed and cleaned
1 tablespoon garlic oil (see page 63)

Place the tapioca in a large bowl. Add the hot water and mix thoroughly, first with a wooden spoon and then with clean hands, until the mixture becomes soft and pliable. Form into small balls, about 1 cm (½ inch) across, keeping them moist between damp tea towels.

Rinse the pickled turnip in a colander under running water until most of the salt has been removed. Press the turnip against the sides of the colander to extract as much liquid as possible. Set them aside.

Heat the oil in a wok or frying pan, add the garlic mixture and stir-fry for 2 minutes. Stir in the minced chicken and stir-fry for 5 minutes more. Add the turnip, onion, nam pla and sugar and stir-fry until most of the liquid has been absorbed, and the mixture can be formed into balls. Remove the pan from the heat and set aside until mixture is cool enough to handle.

Flatten the tapioca balls and place 1 to 1½ tea-spoons of the chicken filling in the centre of each. Re-form the balls around the filling and arrange the balls, well spaced, in 1 or 2 greased steamers, set over boiling water. Steam for 15 minutes.

Arrange a bed of lettuce and spring onions on a large platter, add the steamed tapioca balls and sprinkle lightly with garlic oil. Serve immediately.

Variation: Finely minced pork may be used instead of chicken if preferred.

Sweetcorn Soup

Soup Khow Pode

4 tablespoons chicken stock or water
50 g (2 oz) crab meat or raw prawns, shelled, deveined and finely chopped (see page 63)
1 × 298 g (11 oz) can cream-style corn, drained
1 teaspoon salt
¼ teaspoon freshly ground black pepper
120 ml (4 fl oz) single cream

Place the stock in a medium saucepan and bring to the boil. Stir in the crab meat or prawns.

Add the corn, salt and pepper and allow the mixture to return to the boil, stirring constantly. As soon as it boils, remove from the heat, stir in the cream and serve.

Chicken and Coconut Soup

Gai Tom Khar

1 litre (1¾ pints) coconut milk
20 slices galanga (khar root), shredded
4 makrut (citrus) leaves
2 teaspoons salt
2 tablespoons nam pla (fish gravy)
500 g (1 lb) chicken breast, finely shredded
120–250 ml (4–8 fl oz) chicken stock or water
2 tablespoons lemon juice
4 Thai chillies, crushed
chopped fresh coriander leaves, to garnish

Bring the coconut milk to the boil in a large saucepan.

Stir in the galanga, makrut leaves, salt, nam pla and chicken and return the milk to the boil. Lower the heat and simmer for 15 to 20 minutes, or until the chicken is cooked, adding a little chicken stock or water if the soup is too rich.

Remove the pan from the heat, add the lemon juice and chillies, and transfer to a serving bowl. Garnish with chopped coriander leaves and serve.

Above: Hot and Sour Prawn Soup; right: Sweetcorn Soup

Hot and Sour Prawn Soup

Tom Yum Gung

750 ml (1¼ pints) chicken stock or water
4 takrai (lemon grass) stems
4 makrut (citrus) leaves
1 teaspoon salt
4 tablespoons nam pla (fish gravy)
225 g (8 oz) button mushrooms, wiped and sliced
400 g (14 oz) raw prawns, deveined (see page 63)
4 tablespoons single cream
2 tablespoons lemon juice
4 small Thai chillies, finely crushed
2 teaspoons paprika oil (see page 63)
chopped fresh coriander, to garnish

Place the stock and takrai in a large saucepan and bring to the boil. Add the makrut leaves, salt and nam pla. Stir well.

Add the mushrooms and cook over moderate heat for 3 minutes, then add the prawns and cook for 2 minutes, or until they turn pink. The prawns must not be overcooked or they will toughen.

Lower the heat and stir in the cream. Cook gently for 1 minute, stirring occasionally, taking care that the liquid does not boil.

Remove the soup from the heat and add the lemon juice, chillies and paprika oil. Transfer to a deep serving bowl, garnish with coriander leaves and serve immediately.

Note: In Thailand, takrai is cut in 2.5 cm (1 inch) lengths and crushed. Its distinctive aroma is essential to many Thai dishes.

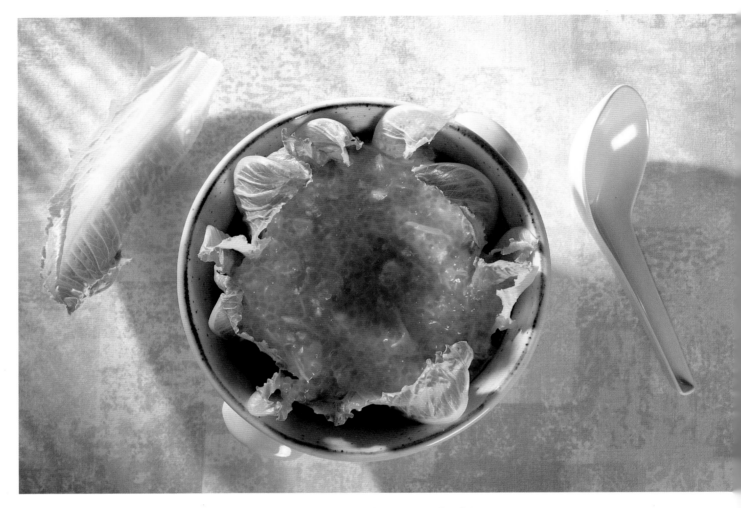

Left: Clear Tapioca Soup; right: Hot Seafood Soup

Clear Vermicelli Soup

Kang Choud Wun Sen

2 tablespoons vegetable oil
2 teaspoons garlic mixture (see page 62)
225 g (8 oz) minced pork
1 litre (1¾ pints) chicken stock or water
100 g (4 oz) vermicelli
4 spring onions, cut in 2.5 cm (1 inch) lengths
½ medium onion, shredded
2 tablespoons nam pla (fish gravy)
2 teaspoons salt or 1 chicken stock cube, crumbled
225 g (8 oz) raw prawns, shelled and deveined (see page 63)
2 sticks celery with leaves, sliced

To garnish:
fresh coriander leaves
freshly ground black pepper

Heat the oil in a large saucepan. Add the garlic mixture and stir-fry for 1 minute.

Add the minced pork and stir-fry for 3 minutes, then add the stock and bring to the boil. Stir in the vermicelli,

spring onions, onion, nam pla and salt, return the soup to the boil and cook for 3 minutes. Lower the heat, add the prawns and celery and simmer for 2 minutes more.

Transfer to a serving bowl, garnish with coriander leaves and a sprinkling of black pepper and serve.

Clear Bean Curd Soup

Kang Choud Tau Fu

1 litre (1¾ pints) water
1 vegetable stock cube
225 g (8 oz) minced pork
1 × 297 g (10½ oz) package bean curd, cut into large squares
100 g (4 oz) fresh bean sprouts, trimmed
4 tablespoons nam pla (fish gravy)
2 spring onions, chopped
1 stick celery with leaves, chopped
freshly ground black pepper

Bring the water to the boil in a large saucepan. Crumble in the stock cube and stir well.

Place the minced pork in a bowl, add about 250 ml (8 fl oz) of the hot stock and stir with a fork to break up

This is a popular Thai snack, which may also be served as part of a main meal.

Bring the stock or water to the boil in a large saucepan. Crumble in the stock cube and stir well.

Place the minced pork in a bowl, add about 120 ml (4 fl oz) of the hot stock, and stir with a fork to break up the meat.

Add the pork mixture to the stock in the pan with the nam pla and cook over moderate heat for 5 minutes. Add the tapioca and cook for about 15 minutes or until the tapioca is clear and cooked through. Add the crab meat and stir thoroughly so that the ingredients are well blended.

Line a serving bowl or soup tureen with lettuce leaves and pour the soup into it. Stir in the garlic oil, coriander leaves and pepper to taste, disturbing the lettuce leaves as little as possible. Serve immediately.

Hot Seafood Soup

Poah Tag

4 makrut (citrus) leaves
750 ml (1¼ pints) chicken stock or water
1 tablespoon cooked red curry paste (see page 63)
1 teaspoon salt
2 tablespoons nam pla (fish gravy)
4 takrai (lemon grass) stems, finely chopped
5 slices galanga (khar root), shredded
100 g (4 oz) cod fillet
100 g (4 oz) raw prawns, shelled and deveined (see page 63)
100 g (4 oz) crab claws
100 g (4 oz) squid (see page 63)
100 g (4 oz) shelled mussels
4 Thai chillies, crushed
2 tablespoons lemon juice

To garnish:
1 tablespoon finely chopped fresh mint
1 tablespoon finely chopped fresh coriander

Remove the central ribs from the makrut leaves, dividing the leaves in half. Set aside.

Mix 2 tablespoons of the stock with the curry paste in a small saucepan. Heat the mixture, stirring, until it forms a sauce. Keep warm until required.

Bring the remaining stock to the boil in a large saucepan. Stir in salt, nam pla, takrai, makrut leaves and galanga.

Add the fish and shellfish to the stock, return the stock to the boil, then lower the heat slightly and cook for 5 minutes.

Stir in the curry sauce with the chillies and lemon juice, and transfer the soup to a serving bowl or soup tureen.

Garnish with chopped mint and coriander leaves and serve.

21

the meat so that there are no lumps.

Add the pork mixture to the stock in the pan and cook over moderate heat for 5 minutes. Stir in the bean curd, bean sprouts, nam pla, spring onions and celery and celery leaves and bring to the boil. Lower the heat and simmer for 3 minutes more.

Transfer to a serving bowl or soup tureen, sprinkle with pepper and serve on its own as a starter or as an accompaniment to the main meal, in the traditional Thai way.

Clear Tapioca Soup

Kang Choud Sa-Koo

1 litre (1¾ pints) chicken stock or water
1 vegetable stock cube
100 g (4 oz) minced pork
2 tablespoons nam pla (fish gravy)
75 g (3 oz) tapioca, washed and drained
75 g (3 oz) crab meat
1 lettuce, separated into leaves
2 tablespoons garlic oil (see page 63)
1 tablespoon chopped fresh coriander leaves
freshly ground black pepper

Fish & Shellfish

There are many fish and shellfish dishes in Thai cuisine. This is no surprise given that Thailand enjoys the warm, fish-rich waters of the Gulf of Siam along the length of its coastline. Prawns, squid and shellfish are especially plentiful, and there are a number of memorable seafood recipes in this chapter. Although many of the fish eaten in Thailand are not found in Western seas, the imaginative treatment they receive means that the recipes adapt well for fish of all sorts.

As in most other South-East Asian countries, meat and fish are mixed freely in Thai dishes as their flavours are felt to be complementary. (This is echoed in the use of nam pla – fish gravy – with meat, poultry and game.) Pork, in particular, features in a number of the recipes in this chapter.

Prawns with Curry Topping

Gung Rard Prig

8 raw Pacific prawns, shelled and deveined (see page 63)
1 teaspoon garlic mixture (see page 62)
oil for deep-frying
3 tablespoons vegetable oil
1 tablespoon red curry paste (see page 63)
1 tablespoon nam pla (fish gravy)
1½ tablespoons sugar
1 tablespoon ground dried prawns

To garnish:
1 teaspoon finely shredded makrut (citrus) leaves
1 teaspoon finely shredded red chilli

Combine the prawns and garlic mixture and stir well to mix. Cover the prawns and set aside to marinate for 10 to 15 minutes.

Heat the oil in a wok or deep-fat fryer and deep-fry the prawns for 4 to 5 minutes until golden brown.

Remove the prawns with a slotted spoon and drain on paper towels. Transfer to a serving dish and keep warm.

To make the topping, heat the vegetable oil in a frying pan. Add the curry paste and cook, stirring, for 2 minutes. Stir in the nam pla, sugar and dried prawns and cook, stirring constantly, for 2 minutes more.

Pour the curry topping over the prawns, garnish with shredded makrut leaves and chilli and serve immediately.

Variation: 1 medium John Dory, red mullet or mackerel may be used instead of the prawns, if preferred. Score the skin of the fish two or three times to allow it to absorb the marinade.

Left: Prawns in Oyster Sauce with Broccoli; right: Seafood in Batter with plum sauce

Seafood in Batter

Gung Pla Choob Pang Tod

1 teaspoon garlic mixture (see page 62)
1 teaspoon nam pla (fish gravy)
100 g (4 oz) mixed fish or shellfish (see Note)
175 ml (6 fl oz) tempura batter (see page 62)
oil for deep-frying
8 string beans
1 green pepper, cored, seeded and cut into 8 pieces
1 large carrot, quartered lengthwise
4 baby corn cobs
plum sauce, to serve (see page 62)

Combine the garlic mixture, nam pla and fish or shellfish in a shallow dish. Marinate for 5 minutes.

Prepare the tempura batter in a medium bowl. Heat the oil in a wok or deep-fat fryer.

Dip the vegetables, one by one, in the batter, and deep-fry until puffed and golden. Drain on paper towels.

Cook the fish or shellfish in the same way. Do not cook too much at once, or the temperature of the oil will fall and the results will be unsatisfactory.

Transfer the cooked fish and vegetables to a serving plate and serve immediately, with plum sauce.

Note: Any type of firm fish or shellfish may be used for this recipe. Filleted fish should be cut in 1 cm (½ inch)

thick slices; squid should be cleaned and cut in 1 cm (½ inch) rings and crab claws should be shelled. Instructions for the preparation of fresh prawns are given on page 63.

Prawns in Oyster Sauce with Broccoli

Gung Bhud Broccoli Nam Mun Hoi

2 tablespoons vegetable oil
1–2 cloves garlic, crushed
100 g (4 oz) raw prawns, shelled and deveined (see page 63)
½ teaspoon freshly ground black pepper
1 tablespoon oyster sauce
100 g (4 oz) broccoli, trimmed and sliced
tablespoons fish or vegetable stock, or water

In Thailand, this dish is often made with vegetables alone as an accompaniment to meat and fish dishes.

Heat the oil in a wok, add the garlic and stir-fry until golden. Add the prawns, pepper and oyster sauce and stir-fry for 2 minutes.

Stir in the broccoli and stock and cook for 3 minutes more. Serve hot with boiled rice.

Variation: Fillet steak may be used instead of prawns.

Prawns with Vermicelli

Gung Ob Moh Din

100 g (4 oz) belly of pork or 6 rashers streaky bacon,
rinded and shredded
3 coriander stems
3 cloves garlic, lightly crushed
1 × 5 cm (2 inch) piece root ginger, crushed
1 tablespoon whole black peppercorns
100 g (4 oz) vermicelli, soaked in boiling water until
soft, and then cut in 1 cm (½ inch) lengths
2 red chillis
8 raw Pacific prawns, deveined (see page 63)
1 tablespoon oyster sauce
250 ml (8 fl oz) chicken stock or water

Line the bottom of a flameproof casserole with the pork or bacon. Strew the coriander stems, garlic, ginger and peppercorns on top and add a layer of vermicelli and red chillis.

Arrange the prawns on top of the vermicelli, sprinkling them with oyster sauce. Pour in the stock, taking care not to disturb the prawns, cover tightly and cook over high heat for 15 minutes. Serve immediately, with nam pla (fish gravy), if liked.

Crab in the Shell

Bhou Jah

4 crab shells, washed and dried
2 tablespoons fresh coriander leaves
strips of red chilli
2 eggs
oil for deep-frying
chilli sauce or nam pla (fish gravy), to serve

Filling:
75 g (3 oz) crab meat
75 g (3 oz) minced raw prawns (see page 63)
225 g (8 oz) minced pork
1 egg
1 tablespoon garlic mixture (see page 62)
1 tablespoon nam pla (fish gravy)
1 tablespoon soy sauce

First prepare the filling. Mix the crab meat, prawns and pork in a small bowl. Stir in the egg, garlic mixture, nam pla and soy sauce.

Pack the crab shells with the shellfish and pork mixture and place in the top of a steamer. Strew with coriander leaves and strips of red chilli.

Place the steamer over boiling water and steam the filled crabs for 15 minutes. Set aside until cool.

Beat the eggs in a shallow bowl. Heat the oil in a wok or deep-fat fryer. Dip each crab, filled side down, in the egg and deep-fry for 1 to 2 minutes or until the egg coating is golden. Remove the crabs with a slotted spoon, drain on paper towels and transfer to a serving dish. Serve with chilli sauce or nam pla.

Stuffed Squid

Pla Mhouk Sord Sai

16 baby squid, cleaned (see page 63)
200 g (7 oz) minced pork
½ teaspoon garlic mixture (see page 62)
1 tablespoon nam pla (fish gravy)
1 egg, beaten
25 g (1 oz) dried breadcrumbs
oil for deep-frying
chilli sauce, to serve

Prepare each squid as instructed on page 63, reserving the heads.

Place the pork in a bowl with the garlic mixture and nam pla and mix well. Fill each squid with this mixture and replace the heads, securing them in place with wooden cocktail sticks.

With a skewer or sharp cocktail stick, pierce the skin around the tail of each squid in 2 or 3 places to let out air while the squid are cooking.

Arrange the stuffed squid in the top of a large steamer. Place over boiling water and steam for 10 minutes. Allow the squid to cool, then remove the wooden cocktail sticks. Put the beaten egg in one shallow dish and the breadcrumbs in another. Heat the oil in a wok or deep-fat fryer. Dip each stuffed squid in egg and breadcrumbs and deep-fry until crisp. Drain on paper towels and serve immediately with chilli sauce. **Variation:** Steamed stuffed squid may also be stir-fried with garlic mixture and nam pla (fish gravy).

Spicy Fried Fishcakes

Tod Mun Pla

500 g (1 lb) cod fillet, skinned and cut in chunks
3 tablespoons red curry paste (see page 63)
1 egg
3 tablespoons nam pla (fish gravy)
75 g (3 oz) green beans, finely chopped
1 tablespoon finely shredded makrut (citrus) leaves
oil for shallow frying

Combine the fish and the curry paste in a food processor or blender, and process until the fish is finely chopped. (This may be done in a mortar with a pestle if preferred.)

Transfer the fish mixture to a bowl and add the egg and nam pla. Knead with clean hands to make a stiff mixture. Work in the beans and makrut leaves in the same way.

Form the mixture into 16 to 20 balls and flatten each to a round about 1 cm (½ inch) thick. Heat the oil in a large frying pan and fry the fishcakes for 4 to 5 minutes on each side over medium heat. Do not allow the fishcakes to overcook, or they will dry out.

Drain the fishcakes on paper towels, transfer to a serving plate and serve hot with cucumber salad (see page 53), enlivened by the addition of a few crushed, roasted peanuts and dressed with chilli sauce.

24

Above: Crab in the Shell with chilli sauce; Spicy Fried Fishcakes with cucumber salad

25

Fish in Garlic Sauce

Pla Tod Kra Tium Prig Tai

1 medium whole fish (mullet, lemon sole or John
Dory), cleaned
oil for deep-frying
3 tablespoons vegetable oil
2 tablespoons garlic mixture (see page 62)
2 tablespoons nam pla (fish gravy)
1 teaspoon sugar
2 sticks celery, sliced
fresh coriander leaves, to garnish

Pat the fish dry with paper towels. Heat the oil in a wok
or deep-fat fryer and deep-fry the fish for 10 to 15
minutes until golden brown. Using 2 spoons, carefully
remove the fish from the oil and drain on paper towels.

Meanwhile heat the vegetable oil in a saucepan
large enough to hold the fish in a single layer. Stir in the
garlic mixture and cook until it changes colour. Add the
nam pla and stir in the sugar. Place the fish in the pan,
turning it over until well coated in the sauce.

Transfer the fish to a serving dish and keep warm.
Add the celery to the sauce remaining in the pan and
stir-fry for 2 minutes, then pour the mixture over
the fish. Garnish with coriander leaves and serve.
Variation: Prawns, squid, pork and chicken can all be
cooked with garlic mixture. For every 225 g (8 oz) meat
or shellfish combine 1 tablespoon garlic mixture, 1
tablespoon nam pla and ½ teaspoon sugar in a shallow
dish. Add the meat or shellfish and marinate for 10
minutes. Cook under a preheated grill or on a barbecue.

Fish in Tamarind Sauce

Pla Rard Prig

1 medium whole John Dory or lemon sole
oil for deep-frying

Tamarind sauce:
3 tablespoons vegetable oil
2–3 cloves garlic, crushed
1–2 chillies, or to taste, finely chopped
120 ml tamarind juice (see page 62)
1 tablespoon nam pla (fish gravy)
3 tablespoons brown sugar

To garnish:
fresh coriander leaves
strips of chilli

Grilled Fish, with vegetable sauce and lemon slices

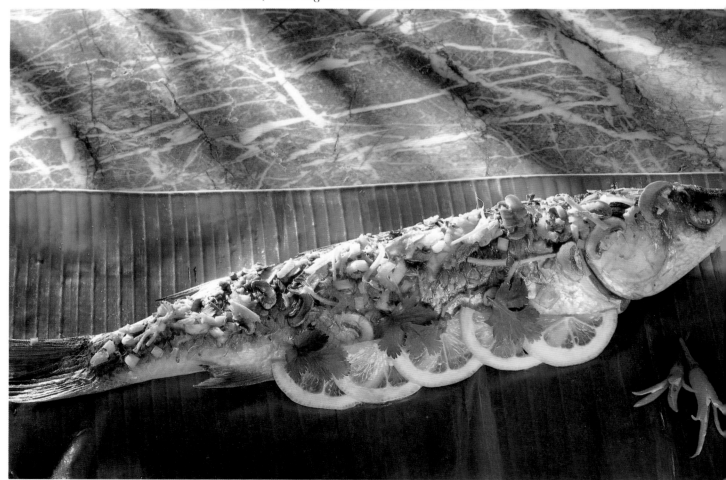

Pat the fish dry with paper towels. Heat the oil in a wok or deep-fat fryer and deep-fry the fish for 10 to 15 minutes or until golden brown. Using 2 spoons, carefully remove the fish from the oil and drain on paper towels. Transfer to a serving dish and keep warm.

Meanwhile make the sauce. Heat the vegetable oil in a small saucepan, add the garlic and chilli and fry, stirring, for 2 minutes. Stir in the tamarind juice, nam pla and brown sugar and bring the liquid to the boil. Boil for 3 minutes, stirring constantly.

Pour the sauce over the fish, and garnish.

Steamed Fish

Pla Pah Sah

1 medium whole grey mullet, cleaned
2 pickled plums, with 2 tablespoons juice from jar
2 tablespoons finely shredded root ginger
40 g (1½ oz) shredded cabbage
2 sticks celery, sliced
3 spring onions, chopped
1 red chilli, shredded
2 pickled garlic, with 2 tablespoons juice from the jar
250 ml (8 fl oz) fish stock or water
strips of lemon rind, to garnish

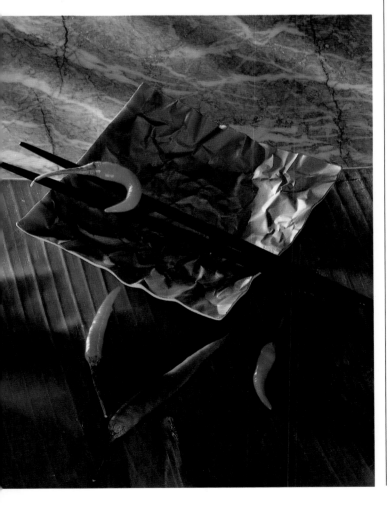

In Thailand, steaming is a popular method of cooking. For this recipe a special pah sah dish would be used over a charcoal stove, but any shallow heatproof dish that will fit inside a steamer will do as well.

Arrange the fish on the plate, with the backbone uppermost. With a needle, prick the fish all over the back area.

Break the pickled plums open and arrange them on top of the fish. Dribble the juice over. Set the plate in the steamer and cook over boiling water for 15 minutes.

Meanwhile, combine the ginger, cabbage, celery, spring onions and chilli in a saucepan. Crush the pickled garlic and add to the pan with the juice from the jar. Stir in the stock.

Bring the liquid to the boil, then pour it over the fish. Continue steaming for 10 minutes more.

Serve the steamed fish hot, garnished with strips of lemon rind.

Grilled Fish

Pla Bhao

1 medium grey mullet, cleaned
½ tablespoon garlic mixture (see page 62)
½ medium onion, chopped
5 mushrooms, wiped and sliced
2 tablespoons shredded root ginger
1 stick celery, sliced
1 teaspoon freshly ground black pepper
1 tablespoon tao chiew (salted soya bean flavouring)
1 tablespoon oyster sauce
250 ml (8 fl oz) fish stock or water

To serve:
1 lettuce, separated into leaves
3 slices lemon

Place the fish on a wooden board and score the skin two or three times with a sharp knife to allow the sauce to be absorbed during cooking. Rub the fish with garlic mixture, pressing this well into the cuts. Transfer the fish to a shallow heatproof dish.

In a bowl, mix all the remaining ingredients well and pour over the fish. Cook under a preheated grill for 20 minutes, turning the fish over halfway through the cooking time.

Just before serving, arrange a bed of lettuce on a shallow serving dish. Carefully transfer the fish to the dish, pour over the vegetable sauce and garnish with the lemon slices. Serve immediately.

Note: This dish is equally delicious when cooked on a barbecue. Score the fish as suggested above and place it on a sheet of foil large enough to enclose it. Rub 1 tablespoon of garlic mixture into the fish, sprinkle with 1 tablespoon oyster sauce, and close the foil to make a package. Cook over coals for about 10 minutes per 500 g (1 lb). Serve with lemon sauce, made by combining 2 tablespoons lemon juice, 1 teaspoon salt, 2 crushed cloves garlic, 2 chopped Thai chillies and ½ tablespoon chopped fresh coriander leaves.

27

Fish with Ginger and Soya Flavouring

Pla Jian

2 medium grey mullet or mackerel, cleaned
oil for deep-frying
2 tablespoons vegetable oil
2 cloves garlic, crushed
2 tablespoons shredded root ginger
1 tablespoon tao chiew (salted soya bean flavouring)
1 tablespoon sugar
1 teaspoon nam pla (fish gravy)
½ teaspoon freshly ground black pepper
250 ml (8 fl oz) fish stock or water
5 spring onions, sliced

To garnish:
fresh coriander leaves
strips of red chilli

Cut the fish into large chunks and pat dry on paper towels. Heat the oil in a wok or deep-fat fryer and deep-fry the fish for 10 to 15 minutes until golden brown. Remove the fish with a slotted spoon and drain on paper towels.

Heat the vegetable oil in a saucepan large enough to hold the fish chunks in a single layer. Stir in the garlic and cook until pale gold in colour. Add the ginger, tao chiew, sugar, nam pla and pepper and stir well.

Stir in the stock and bring the liquid to the boil. Add the fried fish and spring onions, lower the heat and simmer for 10 minutes.

Serve hot, garnished with coriander leaves and strips of red chilli.

Sour Fish Curry

Kang Som Pla

350 ml (12 fl oz) water
150 g (5 oz) cod fillet, sliced
2 tablespoons nam pla (fish gravy)
1 tablespoon sugar
2 tablespoons tamarind juice (see page 62) or lemon juice
175 g (6 oz) mixed vegetables (see Note)

Kang som paste:
6 fresh or dried red chillies, seeded and sliced
⅔ tablespoon salt
1 tablespoon chopped shallots
⅔ tablespoon kapee (shrimp paste)

First make the kang som paste. If using dried chillies, soak them in cold water for 10 minutes and squeeze out as much liquid as possible. Place the chillies in a mortar with the salt and pound to a paste. Add the shallots and kapee and continue to grind the mixture until smooth.

Bring the measured water to the boil in a medium saucepan. Add half the fish, lower the heat and simmer for 5 minutes.

Using a slotted spoon, transfer the fish to a blender. Add the kang som paste and blend until thick and smooth. Alternatively, pound the mixture in a mortar with a pestle.

Place the fish paste in the washed and dried saucepan and bring to the boil over moderate heat. Stir in the nam pla, sugar, tamarind juice or lemon juice.

Add the vegetables and remaining fish, stir well, cover and simmer for 10 minutes. Serve immediately.
Note: Cauliflower, cabbage, courgettes and green beans are all suitable for this curry.
Variation: Shelled and deveined prawns may be used instead of cod fillets, if preferred.

Crab Curry

Poo Bhud Bhong Ka Rhee

1 × 450 g (1 lb) crab
1 teaspoon curry powder
250 ml (8 fl oz) water
4 spring onions, cut into 4 cm (1½ inch) lengths
2 red chillies, seeded and shredded
1½ teaspoons sugar
1 tablespoon white wine
½ teaspoon salt
¼ teaspoon freshly ground black pepper
1 egg
1 tablespoon single cream

To prepare the crab, remove the legs and claws and set aside. Remove the undershell and discard the gills. Clean the body of the crab and cut the meat into small chunks. Crack the legs and claws, extract the meat and cut it into similar-sized chunks. Set the crabmeat aside.

Mix the curry powder with the water in a medium saucepan and bring to the boil.

Stir in the reserved crabmeat. Allow the liquid to return to the boil and add the spring onions, shredded chilli, sugar, wine, salt and pepper. Lower the heat and simmer for 10 minutes.

Meanwhile combine the egg and cream in a small bowl. Mix well, beat in 2 tablespoons of the curry sauce and return the mixture to the saucepan. Stir over gentle heat for b minute, transfer to a serving bowl and serve immediately.

Left: Sour Fish Curry; right: Fish with Ginger and Soya Flavouring

Fish with Tamarind Juice and Ginger

Tom Som Pla

2 medium grey mullet or mackerel, cleaned
4 red shallots, chopped, or 4 tablespoons chopped onion
1 tablespoon kapee (shrimp paste)
1 teaspoon freshly ground black pepper
750 ml (1¼ pints) water
2 tablespoons shredded root ginger, washed
2 tablespoons tamarind juice (see page 62)
4 tablespoons nam pla (fish gravy)
3 tablespoons brown sugar
4 spring onions, chopped

Remove the head from each mullet or mackerel and cut the fish in half.

Grind the shallots or onion in a mortar with the kapee and pepper until the ingredients are thoroughly blended and the mixture forms a paste. Stir the paste into the water in a saucepan large enough to take the pieces of fish and bring to the boil.

Add the fish, ginger, tamarind juice, nam pla, brown sugar and spring onions. Lower the heat and simmer for 20 minutes. Serve hot.

Meat & Poultry

While it would be a simplification to say that Thai cookery brings together the best of Chinese and Indian traditions, there is an element of truth in such a view, as the range of dishes in this chapter suggests. The bright colours, crisp textures and fresh flavours of the earlier dishes evoke China, while the rich warmth and voluptuous textures of the final curries look west to India.

Such a view, though, does not take into account the distinctively Thai elements in the dishes: the use of fish, citrus and coconut flavours with meat, the use of herbs in preference to spices, and beautiful presentation are all authentically Thai.

30

Chicken with Cashew Nuts

Gai Bhud Med Ma Maung

3½ tablespoons vegetable oil
½ tablespoon chopped dried red chilli
1 small clove garlic, crushed
100 g (4 oz) chicken breast, skinned and thinly sliced
¼ teaspoon freshly ground black pepper
1 tablespoon nam pla (fish gravy)
1 teaspoon sugar
1 canned pineapple ring, chopped
4 spring onions, sliced
2 tablespoons chopped green pepper
100 g (4 oz) cashew nuts

In a small frying pan, heat ½ tablespoon of the oil and fry the dried red chilli until crisp. Drain on paper towels and set aside.

Heat the remaining oil in a wok. Add the garlic and stir-fry until golden. Add the chicken, pepper, nam pla and sugar, stirring constantly for 6 to 8 minutes, until the chicken is tender.

Add the pineapple, spring onions and green pepper and stir-fry for 2 minutes more. Finally add the cashew nuts and fried chilli and stir through quickly. Serve hot with boiled rice.

Grilled Chicken, Sala Thai Style

Gai Yang

8 chicken drumsticks
2 tablespoons garlic mixture (see page 62)
1 teaspoon salt
2 tablespoons dark soy sauce
3 tablespoons honey
2 teaspoons ground ginger
1 tablespoon oyster sauce

In Thailand, this is traditionally served with steamed sticky or glutinous rice and Thai Sweet and Sour Salad (see page 51).

Place the chicken drumsticks on a wooden board and pierce them all over with a fork.

Combine all the remaining ingredients in a shallow dish large enough to hold the drumsticks in a single layer. Add the drumsticks and turn to coat well. Cover and set aside to marinate for at least 2 hours.

Grill the marinated drumsticks on a barbecue over medium hot coals for 30 minutes, turning the chicken over halfway through, or cook under a conventional grill. Serve immediately.

Above: Chicken with Baby Corn Cobs; below: Grilled Chicken, Sala Thai Style with Thai Sweet and Sour Salad

Chicken with Baby Corn Cobs

Bhud Khow Pode Orn

2 tablespoons vegetable oil
1 small clove garlic, crushed
100 g (4 oz) chicken breast, skinned and thinly sliced
¼ teaspoon freshly ground black pepper
1 tablespoon nam pla (fish gravy)
½ teaspoon sugar
2 canned pineapple rings, chopped with 2 tablespoons juice from the can
3 spring onions, sliced
100 g (4 oz) fresh or canned baby corn cobs
4 tablespoons chicken stock or water

Heat the oil in a wok. Add the garlic and stir-fry until golden. Add the chicken, pepper, nam pla, sugar, pineapple and juice, stirring constantly.

Stir in the spring onions, corn and stock and cook for 5 minutes. Serve hot, with boiled rice.

Variation: Shelled prawns or sliced pork fillet may be used instead of the chicken.

Chicken in Theoy Leaves

Gai Hoh Bai Theoy

4 chicken thighs
1 tablespoon oyster sauce
1 tablespoon Maggi sauce
1 tablespoon garlic mixture (see page 62)
1 tablespoon whisky
theoy leaves for wrapping
oil for deep-frying

Bone the chicken thighs and divide each thigh into 4 pieces. Combine the oyster sauce, Maggi sauce, garlic mixture and whisky in a shallow dish large enough to hold the chicken in a single layer. Add the chicken and turn to coat well. Cover and set aside to marinate for at least 2 hours.

Wrap each piece of marinated chicken in theoy leaves to make a parcel. Heat the oil in a wok or deep-fat fryer. Fry the chicken parcels, a few at a time, for 15 to 20 minutes, or until golden brown. Drain and serve immediately.

32

Above: Beef with Mushrooms and Oyster Sauce; below: Pork with Chilli and Basil

Stuffed Chicken Wings

Peag Gai Sord Sai

16 chicken wings
300 g (11 oz) minced chicken
100 g (4 oz) vermicelli, softened in boiling water and cut in 1 cm (½ inch) lengths
100 g (4 oz) drained canned water chestnuts, finely chopped
1 tablespoon garlic mixture (see page 62)
1 egg, lightly beaten
2 tablespoons nam pla (fish gravy)
2 tablespoons soy sauce

To prepare the chicken, remove the top part of each wing. The aim is to bone the wings without damaging the skin. Do this by cutting around the bones with a small sharp knife and easing them out, or break the wing joint and work the bones loose with your fingers. Turn the wings inside out to remove the bones.

Make the filling by mixing all the remaining ingredients together in a bowl. Stir well. Carefully stuff each boned chicken wing with a little of the mixture. Place in the top of a large steamer and steam over boiling water for 20 minutes — you may need to do this in several batches. When the wings are cooked, set them aside to cool.

The chicken wings may be used in a variety of ways. Try them stir-fried with garlic mixture and nam pla; or marinated in garlic mixture and nam pla and then barbecued. They are equally tasty coated in egg and breadcrumbs, deep-fried and served with sweet and sour or chilli sauce.

If you want to prepare the chicken wings in advance, they can be frozen most successfully.

Sweet and Sour Pork

Bhud Priew Wharn

2 tablespoons vegetable oil
1 small clove garlic, crushed
100 g (4 oz) pork fillet, thinly sliced
¼ teaspoon freshly ground black pepper
1 tablespoon nam pla (fish gravy)
1 teaspoon sugar
½ cucumber, shredded
3 spring onions, chopped
1 medium tomato, chopped
1 canned pineapple ring, chopped
1 tablespoon tomato sauce
4 tablespoons chicken or vegetable stock, or water

Heat the oil in a wok. Add the garlic and stir-fry until golden. Add the pork, pepper, nam pla and sugar. Stir-fry for 6 to 8 minutes, or until the pork is cooked.

Stir in all the vegetables, with the pineapple, tomato sauce and stock. Cook for 3 minutes more. Serve hot with boiled rice.

Variation: Chicken breast or shelled prawns may be used instead of the pork.

Pork with Chilli and Basil

Bhud Prig-Noh Mai

2 tablespoons vegetable oil
1 clove garlic, crushed
2 chillies, or to taste, finely chopped
100 g (4 oz) pork fillet, thinly sliced
¼ teaspoon freshly ground black pepper
1 tablespoon nam pla (fish gravy)
½ teaspoon sugar
50 g (2 oz) bamboo shoots, shredded (optional)
2 tablespoons finely chopped onion
2 tablespoons shredded green pepper
4 tablespoons chicken or vegetable stock, or water
4 tablespoons fresh basil leaves

Heat the oil in a wok. Add the garlic and chilli and stir-fry until the garlic is golden. Add the pork, pepper, nam pla and sugar, stirring constantly.

Stir in the bamboo shoots, if using, with the onion, green pepper and stock. Cook for 5 minutes. Stir in the basil leaves and cook for 1 minute more. Serve immediately with boiled rice.

Variation: Fillet or rump steak, chicken breast or shelled prawns may be used instead of pork. If bamboo shoots are omitted, the dish is called Bhud Kra Prau.

Beef with Mushrooms and Oyster Sauce

Nauh Bhud Num Mun Hoi Hed

1 tablespoon oyster sauce
1 teaspoon cornflour
½ teaspoon freshly ground black pepper
100 g (4 oz) fillet steak, thinly sliced
2 tablespoons vegetable oil
1 small clove garlic, crushed
50 g (2 oz) mushrooms, wiped and sliced
4 spring onions, sliced
4 tablespoons chicken stock or water

Combine the oyster sauce, cornflour and pepper in a shallow dish, add the steak and marinate for 15 minutes.

Heat the oil in a wok, add the garlic and stir-fry until golden. Add the marinated meat and stir-fry for 3 to 4 minutes until medium-done.

Add the mushrooms, spring onions and stock and cook for 2 minutes more. Serve hot with boiled rice.

Note: It is not essential to use fillet steak for this recipe, though the meat must be suitable for stir-frying. If using anything other than fillet steak, increase the marinating time to 1 hour.

Variation: This dish is also very good made with prawns.

33

Beef with Pepper

Nauh Mhug Prig Tai

*500 g (1 lb) rump steak, cut in slices 1 cm (½ inch)
thick
20 peppercorns, roughly ground
1 teaspoon salt
1 tablespoon oyster sauce
1 teaspoon Maggi sauce
1 teaspoon ground ginger
1 clove garlic, crushed
25 g (1 oz) butter, melted
1 tablespoon whisky*

Cut the steak into strips about 3.5 cm (1½ inches) long, 2.5 cm (1 inch) wide and 1 cm (½ inch) thick. Place the strips on a wooden board and pound them with a meat mallet until tender.

Combine all the remaining ingredients in a shallow dish large enough to hold the steak in a single layer. Add the steak and turn in the marinade mixture to ensure that all the strips of meat are thoroughly coated. Cover and set aside to marinate for at least 2 hours.

Grill on a barbecue over medium hot coals for 10 to 15 minutes, turning steak over halfway through cooking time, or cook under a conventional grill.

Serve immediately, with nam pla or chilli sauce and a green salad.

Variation: The marinated steak may also be fried in a little vegetable oil, if preferred.

34

Beef with Ginger and Jelly Mushrooms

Bhud Khing

*100 g (4 oz) jelly mushrooms or fungi
2 tablespoons vegetable oil
1 clove garlic, crushed·
100 g (4 oz) rump steak, thinly sliced
2 tablespoons finely shredded and washed root
ginger
1 tablespoon tao chiew (salted soya bean
flavouring)
¼ teaspoon freshly ground black pepper
1 teaspoon sugar
4 spring onions, cut in 2.5 cm (1 inch) lengths
120 ml (4 fl oz) chicken stock or water*

Soak the jelly mushrooms or fungi in boiling water for 20 minutes. Drain, squeezing out excess liquid, remove stems and slice caps.

Heat the oil in a wok. Add the garlic and stir-fry until golden. Add the steak, ginger, tao chiew, pepper and sugar, stirring constantly. Stir in the jelly mushrooms, spring onions and stock and cook for 5 minutes.

Serve the beef and jelly mushrooms immediately with boiled rice.

Variation: Sliced pork fillet or chicken breast may be used instead of beef.

Steamed Curry in Artichoke Cups

Hoh Mhoke

*8 small globe artichokes
1½ tablespoons nam pla (fish gravy)
150 g (5 oz) minced pork
250 ml (8 fl oz) coconut milk (see page 63)
½ teaspoon cornflour
1½ tablespoons red curry paste (see page 63)
1 egg, beaten
25 g (1 oz) shredded cabbage, blanched
15 g (½ oz) fresh sweet basil leaves
1 tablespoon fresh coriander leaves
½ tablespoon finely shredded makrut (citrus) leaves
½ red chilli, finely shredded*

In Thailand this dish would be served in containers made from banana leaves. However, artichoke cups look equally attractive.

To prepare artichoke cups, begin by pulling away the outer leaves and trimming the base of each artichoke so that it will stand upright. Wash the artichokes in cold water, then cook in boiling water for 3 to 5 minutes. Drain, then cut away and discard the chokes to create edible containers.

To make the curry filling, place the nam pla in a shallow dish, add the minced pork and set aside.

Skim the cream from the top of the coconut milk and measure 3 tablespoons, topping up with coconut milk if necessary. Reserve the remaining milk.

Heat the coconut cream in a small saucepan. Meanwhile place the cornflour in a cup and mix to a paste with 1 teaspoon of the reserved coconut milk.

Stir this paste into the coconut cream and bring the cream to the boil, stirring constantly. When it thickens, remove it from the heat and set aside.

In a large bowl, mix 120 ml (4 fl oz) of the reserved coconut milk with the curry paste. Add the marinated meat, stirring constantly with a wooden spoon so that the meat and milk mixture are thoroughly blended. Stir in the egg and gradually add the rest of the coconut milk.

Mix the blanched cabbage and basil leaves together and divide the mixture between the artichokes. Carefully pour in the curry mixture and top each artichoke with about 1½ teaspoons of the thickened coconut cream.

Carefully place the filled artichokes in the top of one or two steamers, packing them closely together and strewing them with coriander leaves, finely shredded makrut leaves and red chilli.

Place over boiling water and steam for 30 minutes. Using a slotted spoon, carefully transfer the steamed artichokes to a serving platter. Serve immediately.

Note: If globe artichokes are not available, 10 cm (4 inch) foil containers may be used instead.

Variation: Thinly sliced chicken or minced fish may be used instead of pork, if preferred. A mixture of minced fish and shellfish also works well. If using fish or shellfish, add 1 teaspoon minced krachai root to the red curry paste.

Steamed Curry in Artichoke Cups

Chicken Curry

Kang Ka Rhee Gai

2 tablespoons vegetable oil
4 chicken drumsticks
5 shallots or 1 large onion, finely chopped
2 tablespoons plain flour
2 tablespoons curry powder
500 ml (18 fl oz) coconut milk (see page 63)
2 carrots, thinly sliced
4 potatoes, cubed
1 tablespoon nam pla (fish gravy)
½ teaspoon sugar
2 red chillies, seeded and shredded
1 teaspoon salt

Heat the oil in a large saucepan, add the chicken and brown on all sides for 5 minutes. Using tongs, remove the chicken from the pan and reserve.

Add the shallots to the oil remaining in the pan and stir-fry for 2 to 3 minutes until golden.

Stir in the flour and curry powder, cook for 1 minute, then gradually add the coconut milk. Bring to the boil, stirring constantly.

Return the chicken to the pan, with the carrots and potatoes. Stir in the nam pla, sugar, shredded chilli and salt. Lower the heat and simmer for 20 minutes, stirring occasionally. Serve at once.

Chicken Matsaman Curry

Kang Matsaman Gai

3 tablespoons vegetable oil
4 chicken drumsticks
350 ml (12 fl oz) coconut milk
1½ tablespoons matsaman curry paste
3 new potatoes, scrubbed or peeled
1 onion, quartered
½ teaspoon lemon juice
1½ tablespoons nam pla (fish gravy)
½ tablespoon sugar
25 g (1 oz) roasted peanuts

Heat the oil in a large saucepan. Add the chicken and brown on all sides. Stir the coconut milk into the pan and bring it to the boil. Add the curry paste. Lower the heat and simmer for 2 hours.

Stir in the remaining ingredients, cover the pan and simmer for 20 minutes. Serve immediately.
Variation: 750 g (1½ lb) cubed stewing steak may be used instead of chicken.

Red Pork Curry

Kang Bhed Dang Mhoo

1 tablespoon vegetable oil
2 tablespoons red curry paste (see page 63)
225 g (8 oz) pork fillet, thinly sliced
600 ml (1 pint) coconut milk (see page 63)
1 medium aubergine, sliced
2 makrut (citrus) leaves
2 tablespoons nam pla (fish gravy)
1 teaspoon sugar
2 green chillies, seeded and sliced
2 sprigs fresh basil

Heat the oil in a large saucepan over moderate heat. Add the curry paste and stir-fry for 1 minute. Add the pork and stir-fry for 6 to 8 minutes.

Stir in the coconut milk and bring to the boil. Add the aubergine, makrut leaves, nam pla and sugar. Simmer, stirring occasionally, for 15 minutes.

Just before serving, stir in the chillies and basil.
Variation: Chicken may be used instead of pork.

Left: Fried Red Curry with Pork and Beans; right: Chicken Matsaman Curry

Thick Red Beef Curry

Kang Panag Nua

275 g (10 oz) beef brisket, thinly sliced
1 tablespoon vegetable oil
2 tablespoons red curry paste with makrut (see
Variation 2, page 63)
200 ml (⅓ pint) coconut milk
2 makrut (citrus) leaves
1 tablespoon nam pla (fish gravy)
1 tablespoon sugar
2 green chillies, seeded and sliced
2 sprigs fresh basil

Place the beef in a medium saucepan. Add water to
cover and bring to the boil. Lower the heat and simmer
for 1 to 1¼ hours, or until the meat is tender, skimming
the liquid occasionally. Remove the meat with a slotted
spoon and set aside.

Heat the oil in a large saucepan over moderate heat.
Add the curry paste and stir-fry for 1 minute. Stir in 2
tablespoons of the coconut milk and cook, stirring

constantly, for 5 minutes.

Add the cooked beef, makrut leaves, nam pla, sugar
and remaining coconut milk and bring to the boil. Lower
the heat and simmer, stirring occasionally, for 15
minutes. Just before serving, stir in the green chillies
and basil.

Variation: Sliced chicken breast or pork fillet may be
used instead of beef. They will not require pre-cooking.

Fried Red Curry with Pork and Beans

Bhud Prig-Khing Mhoo

175 g (6 oz) green beans (French or runner), cut in 2.5
cm (1 inch) lengths
2 tablespoons vegetable oil
275 g (10 oz) pork fillet, thinly sliced
2 tablespoons red curry paste with dried shrimp (see
Variation 3, page 63)
1 tablespoon nam pla (fish gravy)
1 tablespoon demerara sugar

Place the beans in a medium saucepan. Add water to
cover and bring to the boil. Cook for 5 minutes, then
drain thoroughly in a colander. Set aside.

Heat the oil in a wok, add the pork and stir-fry for 6 to
8 minutes or until the pork is cooked. Using a slotted
spoon, transfer the pork to a plate and reserve. Add the
curry paste to the oil remaining in the pan. Stir-fry for 2
minutes, then return the pork to the pan together with
the nam pla, sugar and cooked beans. Stir-fry for 10
minutes. Serve hot with boiled rice.

37

Chicken, Aubergine and Bamboo Shoot Curry

Kang Pah Gai

3 tablespoons vegetable oil
2 tablespoons red curry paste (see page 63)
275 g (10 oz) chicken breast, thinly sliced
4 tablespoons nam pla (fish gravy)
3 makrut (citrus) leaves
5 krachai roots, finely shredded
600 ml (1 pint) water
3 small green aubergines, quartered
1 × 100 g (4 oz) piece bamboo shoot, finely sliced
2 green chillies, seeded and sliced
2 sprigs fresh basil

Heat the oil in a large saucepan over moderate heat.
Add the curry paste and stir-fry for 1 minute. Add the
chicken, nam pla, makrut leaves and krachai roots and
stir-fry for 5 minutes.

Pour in the measured water and bring to the boil,
then lower the heat and add the aubergine and bamboo
shoot. Stir well. Simmer, stirring occasionally, for 10
minutes. Just before serving, stir in the green chillies
and basil.

Eggs Rice & Noodles

Smooth, creamy-tasting eggs are the perfect foil to the hot, sour flavourings that characterize Thai cooking. You'll find a range of egg dishes in the five recipes given here: several are substantial enough to make meals in their own right.

Noodles and rice, as so often in Asia, are of almost equal importance as Thai staples, with noodles taking precedence for snacks and quick meals. Rice, though, is invariably first choice for meals of any importance. The rice dishes given here are all 'speciality' rice dishes – and some would make meals in their own right – but plain boiled rice should not be overlooked. There is no better accompaniment to the richer Thai fish and meat dishes.

Hard-boiled Eggs with Tamarind Sauce

Khai Loog Kheoy

1 teaspoon vinegar
6 eggs
½–1 tablespoon dried red chilli (optional)
4 tablespoons vegetable oil, plus ½ tablespoon for frying the chilli, if using
4 red shallots, finely chopped
120 ml (4 fl oz) tamarind sauce (see page 62)
2 teaspoons dark soy sauce

This delicious dish is a favourite with Thai children and is often served as an accompaniment to curry dishes. The fried chilli may be omitted if preferred.

Bring a saucepan of water to the boil. Stir in the vinegar. Lower the heat and carefully add the eggs. Boil gently for 5 minutes, then drain and run under cold water until cool. Shell the eggs carefully and set them aside.

If you are using the chilli, heat ½ tablespoon of the oil in a small frying pan and fry the chilli until crisp. Drain on paper towels and reserve.

Heat the remaining oil in a large frying pan, add the eggs and fry, turning constantly with a wooden spoon, until golden brown. With a slotted spoon, remove each egg as it browns and drain on paper towels.

Add the shallots to the oil remaining in the pan and fry until golden brown. Transfer with a slotted spoon to a small dish and keep warm.

Pour away all but 2 tablespoons oil from the pan. Add the tamarind sauce and soy sauce and boil until the mixture thickens.

Meanwhile quarter the eggs lengthways and arrange them on a serving dish. Pour the tamarind sauce over and sprinkle with the fried shallots and fried chilli. Serve immediately.

Left: Hard-boiled Eggs with Tamarind Sauce; right: Stuffed Omelette

Stuffed Omelette

Kai Yud Sai

3 tablespoons vegetable oil
1 clove garlic, crushed
100 g (4 oz) minced pork
freshly ground pepper
1 tablespoon nam pla (fish gravy)
½ tablespoon sugar
100 g (4 oz) onion, finely chopped
1 medium tomato, chopped
3 eggs, beaten
coriander leaves, to garnish

In a saucepan, heat 2 tablespoons of the oil. Add the garlic and stir-fry until golden brown. Add the minced pork, pepper, nam pla, sugar, onion and tomato, and continue to stir-fry for 5 to 10 minutes, until all the ingredients are cooked and well blended.

Heat the remaining oil in a wok, and tilt so that the oil coats the entire surface of the wok. Pour away the excess oil. Pour in the beaten eggs and swirl around the inside of the wok to form a thin skin.

Place the filling in the middle of the omelette, and fold down the 4 sides to make a neat parcel. Turn out on to a serving dish, folded side down, garnish with coriander leaves and serve immediately.

Fried Eggs with Pork Sauce

Khai Dao Rad Nah

3 tablespoons vegetable oil
100 g (4 oz) minced pork
1 small clove garlic, crushed
½ medium onion, finely chopped
1 carrot, diced
1 tablespoon soy sauce
1 teaspoon sugar
2 tablespoons tomato ketchup
½ teaspoon salt
½ teaspoon freshly ground black pepper
120 ml (4 fl oz) water
4 eggs
1 tablespoon chopped coriander leaves, to garnish

Heat 1 tablespoon of the oil in a large frying pan. Add the minced pork and stir-fry for 3 minutes, then add the garlic, onion and carrot and stir-fry the pork and vegetables for 3 minutes more. Stir in the soy sauce, sugar, tomato ketchup, salt and pepper, adding the water gradually to form a thick sauce. Bring to the boil, lower the heat and simmer for 5 minutes. Remove the frying pan from the heat, cover with a lid or foil, and set aside.

Heat the remaining oil in a second large frying pan and fry the eggs. Transfer them to a shallow serving dish, spoon the pork sauce over and serve immediately, garnished with the chopped coriander leaves.

Left: Crispy Rice with Dipping Sauce; right: Pineapple Fried Rice

40

Steamed Egg with Minced Pork

Khai Tune

2 eggs
100 g (4 oz) minced pork
1 small onion, finely chopped
1 teaspoon salt
½ teaspoon freshly ground black pepper
250 ml (8 fl oz) water

To garnish:
1 teaspoon chopped spring onion
1 teaspoon chopped fresh coriander leaves

Place the eggs in a mixing bowl and beat with a rotary whisk or electric mixer until fluffy.

Stir in the pork, onion, salt, pepper and water and mix well.

Spoon the mixture into a heatproof bowl and place in the top of a steamer over boiling water. Steam for 30 minutes.

Serve immediately, garnished with chopped spring onion and coriander.

Minced Pork Omelette

Khai Jiew Moo Sub

2 eggs
100 g (4 oz) minced pork
1 small onion, finely chopped
1 teaspoon garlic mixture (see page 62)
1 teaspoon chopped fresh coriander
½ tablespoon nam pla (fish gravy)
4 tablespoons vegetable oil

Combine all the ingredients except the oil in a mixing bowl and mix well.

Heat the oil in a large frying pan over moderate heat, and add the mixture. Tilt the pan to form an omelette, lifting the sides of the omelette with a knife or spatula so that any liquid egg flows underneath. As soon as the underside of the omelette is cooked (about 4 to 5 minutes), flip it over and cook the other side.

Slide the omelette on to a warm plate and serve immediately.

Fried Rice with Pork

Khow Bhud Mhoo

2 tablespoons vegetable oil
1 clove garlic, crushed
150 g (5 oz) pork fillet, sliced
3 tablespoons light soy sauce
2 eggs
2 tablespoons tomato ketchup
1 tablespoon sugar
1 small onion, sliced
750 g (1½ lb) cooked rice – about 175 g (6 oz) raw weight

To garnish:
¼ cucumber, thinly sliced
1 lemon, cut in wedges
2 tablespoons chopped coriander leaves
1 red chilli, seeded and shredded

Heat the oil in a wok. Add the garlic and stir-fry for 1 minute or until golden brown.

Add the pork with 1 teaspoon light soy sauce. Stir-fry for 5 minutes.

Break the eggs into the wok, stirring vigorously, and cook for 2 minutes. Add the tomato ketchup, sugar, remaining soy sauce, onion and rice and stir-fry for 5 minutes.

Transfer the mixture to a shallow serving dish and garnish with sliced cucumber, lemon wedges, coriander and shredded chilli. Serve immediately.

Variation: Prawns or chicken breast may be used instead of pork.

Pineapple Fried Rice

Khow Bhud Sub-Pa-Rode

4 tablespoons vegetable oil
1 clove garlic, crushed
100 g (4 oz) ham, cubed
1 medium carrot, diced
4 tablespoons raisins
¼ green pepper, cored, seeded and diced
¼ red pepper, cored, seeded and diced
4 tablespoons nam pla (fish gravy)
1 tablespoon sugar
750 g (1½ lb) cooked rice (about 175 g (6 oz) raw rice)
1 teaspoon freshly ground black pepper
4 fresh or canned pineapple rings, diced

To garnish:
5 spring onions, trimmed
4 tablespoons chopped coriander leaves

This simple and very tasty dish may be served with roasted peanuts, if liked.

Heat the oil in a wok. Add the garlic and stir-fry for 1 minute or until golden brown.

Add the ham, carrot, raisins, green and red pepper, nam pla and sugar. Stir-fry for 5 minutes.

Add the rice, pepper and pineapple and cook, stirring constantly, for 5 minutes more.

Transfer to a serving dish, garnish with spring onions and coriander and serve.

Crispy Rice with Dipping Sauce

Khow Tung Nah Tung

225 g (8 oz) glutinous rice
oil for deep-frying

For the sauce:
4 fl oz (120 ml) coconut milk
50 g (2 oz) minced pork
50 g (2 oz) minced prawns (see page 63)
1 teaspoon garlic mixture (see page 62)
1½ tablespoons nam pla (fish gravy)
1½ tablespoons sugar
50 g (2 oz) finely chopped onion
50 g (2 oz) ground roasted peanuts

To garnish:
coriander leaves
crisply fried strips of red chilli

To make this dish, Thai cooks use the sticky layer left at the bottom of the saucepan after cooking rice. Here is a less authentic, but more reliable, method of making this delicious snack.

Place the rice in a saucepan, cover with water and boil until the rice is thoroughly cooked and has become sticky. Drain through a sieve. Spread the rice out in a layer, as thin as possible, on greased baking trays, pressing down well. Leave to dry in a warm place, or a very cool oven, 120°C, 250°F, Gas Mark ½.

When completely dry and firm, remove from the trays with a fish slice or spatula, and break into large pieces.

Heat the oil until very hot and deep-fry the rice pieces until golden – you should hear the grains begin to pop in about 5 seconds. Remove from the oil and drain on paper towels.

To make the sauce, place the coconut milk in a saucepan and bring to the boil. Add the minced pork and prawns, stirring with a wooden spoon to break up any lumps.

Add the garlic mixture, nam pla, sugar, chopped onion and ground peanuts. Mix the ingredients well, reduce the heat and leave the sauce to simmer for 20 minutes, stirring occasionally.

Place in a serving dish, garnish with coriander leaves and strips of red chilli, and serve as a dip with the crispy rice pieces.

41

Spicy Fried Rice

Khow Bhud Khie Mau

100 g (4 oz) minced beef
½ × 415 g (14.6 oz) can red kidney beans, drained
1½ tablespoons nam pla (fish gravy)
1 tablespoon dark soy sauce
4 red chillies, seeded and finely chopped
2–3 cloves garlic, crushed
½ teaspoon salt
2 tablespoons vegetable oil
10 green beans, trimmed and cut in 1 cm (½ inch) lengths
750 g (1½ lb) cooked rice – about 175 g (6 oz) raw weight
1 tablespoon sugar
20 small fresh basil or mint leaves

Combine the minced beef and kidney beans in a shallow dish. Stir in the nam pla and soy sauce, cover and set aside for 30 minutes to allow flavours to blend.

In a small bowl, mix the chillies, garlic and salt together. Heat the oil in a wok or large frying pan, add the chilli mixture and stir fry for 1 minute.

Add the beef mixture and cook, stirring constantly, for 3 minutes. Add the green beans and stir fry for 3 minutes more.

Stir in the rice and sugar and cook, stirring, until the rice is hot and all the ingredients are thoroughly mixed. Taste, and add more nam pla, salt and pepper if necessary.

Transfer the mixture to a serving dish, add the basil or mint leaves and mix well. Serve immediately.

Creamy Rice with Fish

Khom Tom Pla

175 g (6 oz) long-grain rice
1.6 litre (2¾ pints) chicken stock or water plus 2 tablespoons
3 tablespoons vegetable oil
1 tablespoon chopped garlic
500 g (1¼ lb) cod fillets, thinly sliced
2 tablespoons nam pla (fish gravy)
2 tablespoons tung chai (dry preserved Chinese cabbage)
1 teaspoon freshly ground black pepper
2 spring onions, finely chopped
2 sticks celery with leaves, thinly sliced

This fish and rice dish of porridge-like consistency is widely served in Thailand for breakfast, or as a snack at any time of the day.

Rinse the rice several times in a colander. Drain well.

Bring 600 ml (1 pint) of the stock or water to the boil in a large saucepan. Add the rice, then cook for 20 minutes over a low heat, stirring from time to time. The rice should have absorbed most of the liquid. Add the rest of the stock or water, bring back to the boil, then remove from the heat.

Heat the oil in a large frying pan, add the garlic and stir fry for 1 minute until golden. With a slotted spoon, remove the garlic and reserve.

Add the fish to the oil remaining in the pan and stir fry for 4 to 6 minutes, adding the remaining stock if necessary to prevent sticking.

As soon as the fish is cooked, add it to the rice together with the nam pla, tung chai and pepper. Mix well and transfer to a serving dish.

Sprinkle with spring onions, celery and reserved fried garlic and serve immediately.

Variation: Prawns, squid, pork or chicken may be used instead of fish.

Rice with Boiled Chicken

Khow Mun Gai

1 × 1.5 kg (3 lb) chicken, without giblets
2 teaspoons salt
4 pieces coriander root or stem, bruised
1.5 litres (2½ pints) water
750 g (1½ lb) long-grain rice
5 tablespoons vegetable oil
5 cloves garlic, bruised

Tao chiew sauce:
6 tablespoons tao chiew (salted soya bean flavouring)
2 teaspoons dark soy sauce
2 tablespoons white vinegar or lemon juice
2 teaspoons sugar
2 teaspoons finely chopped root ginger
2 chillies, seeded and very finely chopped

To garnish:
½ cucumber, thinly sliced
2 tablespoons chopped coriander leaves

First make the sauce. Mash the tao chiew thoroughly in a small bowl, then add all the remaining ingredients and mix well. Cover and set aside.

Place the chicken in a saucepan large enough to hold it comfortably. Add the salt, bruised coriander and water. Bring the water to the boil, lower the heat and cook for 45 to 60 minutes, spooning off any scum that rises to the surface of the liquid.

When the chicken is cooked, transfer it to a shallow casserole, reserving the cooking liquid in a large saucepan. Keep the chicken warm while you prepare the rice.

Rinse the rice several times in a colander. Drain thoroughly. Heat the oil in a large saucepan, add the garlic and fry over gentle heat until pale cream in colour. Stir in the rice and cook, stirring constantly, for 3 minutes.

Bring the reserved cooking liquid from the chicken to the boil. Add it to the rice mixture, lower the heat and simmer for 15 minutes or until the rice is cooked but not soggy.

Meanwhile carve the chicken. Arrange a bed of rice on a shallow serving dish, top with chicken and garnish with coriander and cucumber. Serve immediately, with tao chiew sauce.

Noodles with Minced Meat Sauce

Geuy Teuw Nah Sub

500 g (1 lb) soaked rice sticks or noodles
2 tablespoons dark soy sauce
4 tablespoons vegetable oil
1 clove garlic, crushed
300 g (11 oz) minced beef
½ tablespoon nam pla (fish gravy)
½ tablespoon curry powder
1 teaspoon sugar
¼ teaspoon freshly ground black pepper
1 tablespoon cornflour
2 tablespoons light soy sauce
1 small onion, chopped
1 tomato, chopped
350 ml (12 fl oz) chicken or vegetable stock

To serve:
1 lettuce, separated into leaves
2 tablespoons chopped coriander leaves

Soak the rice sticks in cold water for at least 2 hours or until soft.

Spread out the rice sticks or noodles on a large shallow dish. Sprinkle with dark soy sauce and mix thoroughly, using chopsticks or 2 spoons, until all the noodles are coated in soy sauce.

Heat 2 tablespoons of the oil in a wok, add the noodles and stir-fry for 3 to 5 minutes (depending on the type of noodle used). Transfer the contents of the wok to a serving dish and keep warm.

Heat the remaining oil in a large saucepan, add the garlic and stir-fry for 1 minute or until golden brown. Add the beef, nam pla, curry powder, sugar and pepper. Stir well.

In a bowl, mix the cornflour to a paste with the light soy sauce and stir the mixture into the pan. Cook for 10 to 15 minutes, stirring frequently, until the beef is cooked and crumbly.

Stir in the onion, tomato and stock and bring to the boil. Lower the heat and simmer for 5 minutes.

Just before serving, arrange a bed of lettuce on a shallow serving dish, top with the noodles and finally add the minced beef mixture. Garnish with coriander and serve immediately.

Left: Creamy Rice with Fish; right: Spicy Fried Rice

Noodle Salad

Khanom Jeen Sarw Narm

½ × 450 g (1 lb) package Japanese somen
1 × 5 cm (2 inch) piece root ginger, peeled
and thinly sliced
3–4 cloves garlic, thinly sliced
2 tablespoons ground shrimp
6 slices fresh pineapple or canned pineapple rings,
finely chopped
3 lemons, sliced
4 tablespoons nam pla (fish gravy)
4 tablespoons sugar

Fish balls:
300 g (11 oz) cod fillets, cooked and flaked (see
Noodles with Fish Curry Topping, page 46)
1 tablespoon red curry paste (see page 63)
1 tablespoon chopped fresh coriander
1 teaspoon salt
1 tablespoon water
250 ml (8 fl oz) thick coconut milk (see Note)

Bring a large saucepan of water to the boil, add the somen and cook for 10 minutes. Drain thoroughly, rinse under cold water and drain again. With clean hands, scoop the somen gently into loose nest shapes, transfer to a large platter and set aside.

Make the fish balls by combining all the ingredients except the coconut milk in a mixing bowl. Form the mixture into 40 small balls and set aside.

Bring the coconut milk to the boil in a medium saucepan and add the fish balls, a few at a time, so that the milk continues to boil. Cook for about 4 to 5 minutes, turning over halfway through cooking. As each ball cooks, remove it with a slotted spoon and drain on a wire rack set over a tray. Allow to cool. Reserve the coconut milk.

To serve, arrange the fish balls on top of the somen and sprinkle with ginger, garlic and ground shrimp. Arrange the pineapple and lemon around the edge of the platter.

Combine the reserved coconut milk with the nam pla and sugar. The flavour should be sweet and sour. Pour the spiced coconut milk over the top of the fish balls and serve at once.

Note: To make the thick coconut milk, combine 250 ml (8 fl oz) boiling water and 300 g (11 oz) desiccated coconut in a bowl. Allow to stand until cold, then strain the milk, pressing the mixture firmly against the side of the strainer to extract as much liquid as possible.

Variation: For a hotter version of this popular dish, add 15 small Thai chillies to the coating sauce.

Left: Fried Noodles with Vegetable and Meat Topping; right: Thai-Style Fried Rice Sticks

Fried Rice Sticks with Meat and Vegetables

Geuy Teuw Bhud See Euw

2 tablespoons vegetable oil
1 clove garlic, crushed
100 g (4 oz) sliced chicken breast, fillet steak, pork fillet, crab meat or deveined shelled prawns (see page 63), or a combination
½ teaspoon freshly ground black pepper
100 g (4 oz) soaked rice sticks or white or yellow noodles
100 g (4 oz) vegetables, such as cauliflower florets, sliced courgettes or whole green beans
2 teaspoons dark soy sauce
2 tablespoons nam pla (fish gravy)
2 tablespoons sugar
1 egg, beaten (optional)

Like chop suey, this is a very adaptable dish. Almost any tender cut of meat may be used, with prawns or crab meat, if liked. Vegetables are equally interchangeable, as are the noodles used. Adjust cooking times to suit the ingredients used.

Heat the oil in a wok and add the garlic. Stir-fry for 1 minute or until golden brown. Add the meat or shellfish, with the pepper. Stir-fry for 4 to 6 minutes.

Add the rice sticks, if using, and cook for 3 minutes, then add vegetables with soy sauce, nam pla, sugar and egg. Mix well and cook for 3 minutes more. If soft noodles are used, add these with vegetables like cauliflower and courgettes. Hard vegetables like carrots will require a longer cooking time.

Fried Noodles with Vegetable and Meat Topping

Geuy Teuw Rard Nah

4 tablespoons vegetable oil
2 cloves garlic, crushed
100 g (4 oz) egg noodles or soaked rice sticks
2 teaspoons dark soy sauce
100 g (4 oz) sliced chicken breast, fillet steak, pork fillet, prepared squid or deveined shelled prawns (see page 63), or a combination
½ teaspoon freshly ground black pepper
2 tablespoons nam pla (fish gravy)
100 g (4 oz) vegetables, such as cauliflower florets, shredded cabbage or sliced broccoli
300 ml (½ pint) chicken or vegetable stock, or water
1 tablespoon cornflour mixed to a paste with 2 tablespoons water
1 tablespoon tao chiew (salted soya bean flavouring)
2 tablespoons sugar
¼ vinegar (optional)

Heat half the oil in a wok. Add half the garlic and stir-fry for 1 minute or until golden brown.

Add the noodles and soy sauce and cook, stirring constantly, for 3 to 5 minutes (depending on whether soft or hard noodles are used). Transfer the contents of the wok to a serving dish and keep warm.

Heat the remaining oil in the wok, add the remaining garlic and stir-fry until golden brown. Add the meat, pepper and nam pla and stir-fry for 5 minutes more. Add the vegetables and stir-fry for 3 minutes more.

Finally stir in the stock, cornflour paste, tao chiew, sugar and vinegar. Bring the liquid to the boil, lower the heat and cook for 3 minutes, stirring constantly.

Pour the thickened sauce over the noodles and serve immediately.

Thai-Style Fried Rice Sticks

Geuy Teuw Bhud Thai

100 g (4 oz) soaked rice sticks
2 tablespoons vegetable oil
1 clove garlic, chopped
100 g (4 oz) chicken breast, thinly sliced
100 g (4 oz) crab meat, cleaned and picked over
100 g (4 oz) raw prawns, shelled and deveined (see page 63)
2 tablespoons nam pla (fish gravy)
2 tablespoons sugar
½ tablespoon lemon juice or tamarind juice (see page 62)
¼ teaspoon freshly ground black pepper
2 tablespoons crushed roasted peanuts
1 tablespoon ground dried shrimp
1 tablespoon chopped preserved radish or turnip
½ teaspoon ground chilli, or to taste
1 egg
2 tablespoons gui chai leaves or spring onion tops
100 g (4 oz) bean sprouts

To serve:
1 lemon, sliced and quartered
50 g (2 oz) fresh bean sprouts

This dish is a meal on its own. In Thailand it would be served for lunch or as a late supper. It is also sold by street vendors.

Soak the rice sticks in cold water for at least 2 hours or until soft.

Heat the oil in a wok. Add the garlic and stir-fry for 1 minute or until golden brown. Add the chicken, crab meat and prawns and stir-fry for 3 minutes. Stir in the drained rice sticks with the nam pla, sugar, lemon juice and pepper. Cook for 1 minute, then add the crushed peanuts, dried shrimp, preserved radish and ground chilli, stirring constantly.

Break the egg into the pan, stirring all the time, then add the gui chai leaves and bean sprouts and stir-fry for 3 minutes more.

If the rice sticks are still hard, add 1 to 2 tablespoons water and cook until all the water has been absorbed.

Transfer to a serving dish and serve with quartered lemon slices and fresh bean sprouts.

45

Noodles with Fish Curry Topping

Khanom Jeen Num Yar

225 g (8 oz) cod fillets
250 ml (8 fl oz) water
1 litre (1¾ pints coconut milk (see page 63)
3 tablespoons red curry paste (see page 63)
50 g (2 oz) krachai root, very finely chopped
or minced
3 tablespoons nam pla (fish gravy)
½ × 450 g (1 lb) package Japanese somen
120 ml (4 fl oz) coconut cream (see page 63)

Accompaniments:
100 g (4 oz) cooked green beans
100 g (4 oz) preserved cabbage
100 g (4 oz) bean sprouts
1 red chilli
25 g (1 oz) fresh sweet basil leaves

Japanese somen are an excellent substitute for Thai noodles and are more readily available than the Thai product.

Prepare the accompaniments. Slice the beans and shred the preserved cabbage. Place in separate bowls. Blanch the bean sprouts in boiling water for 1 minute, drain thoroughly, then place in another bowl. Seed and chop the chilli and pile in the centre of a small plate with the basil leaves around the rim.

Place the fish in a medium saucepan with the water. Bring to the boil, lower the heat and simmer for 8 to 10 minutes or until the fish flakes easily when tested with a fork. Remove the fish with a slotted spoon and reserve the stock. Discard the skin and flake the flesh.

Place the flaked fish in a clean saucepan with the coconut milk. Bring to just below the boiling point and stir in the reserved fish stock.

Combine the curry paste and krachai root in a small bowl. Mix well and add to the fish mixture, together with the nam pla. Simmer for 15 minutes, stirring occasionally.

Meanwhile cook the somen. Bring a large saucepan of water to the boil, add the somen and cook for 10 minutes. Drain thoroughly, rinse under cold water and drain again. With clean hands, scoop the somen gently into loose nest shapes, transfer to a large platter and warm through in a preheated moderate oven, 160°C (325°F), Gas Mark 3.

When the fish curry has thickened, and a thin film of oil appears on the surface, stir in the coconut cream. Bring to the boil, remove from the heat and spoon the curry over the somen. Serve immediately, with the accompaniments.

Crispy Sweet and Sour Rice Vermicelli

Meeh Grob

oil for deep-frying
150g (5 oz) soaked rice vermicelli
6 tablespoons vegetable oil
1 egg, beaten
1 tablespoon sliced shallots
1 tablespoon sliced garlic
50 g (2 oz) raw prawns, shelled, deveined and cut in
half lengthways (see page 63)
50 g (2 oz) chicken breast, thinly sliced
2 tablespoons tamarind juice (see page 62)
4 tablespoons palm sugar or demerara
1 tablespoon tao chiew (salted soya bean
flavouring)
1 tablespoon nam pla (fish gravy)

To garnish:
1 pickled garlic, drained and sliced
1 red chilli, seeded and sliced
2 tablespoons chopped coriander leaves

This dish is usually accompanied by bean sprouts, spring onions and gui chai leaves.

Heat the oil in a wok or deep-fat fryer. It will be ready when a piece of vermicelli, dropped into the wok, pops open instantly.

Deep-fry the vermicelli in batches. As each batch pops and turns a rich creamy colour, remove it from the wok with a slotted spoon or scoop and drain on paper towels. Keep the cooked vermicelli warm in a bowl, but do not cover, or it may become soft.

Heat half the vegetable oil in a medium saucepan. Pour the beaten egg through a colander or strainer into the pan and cook until the strands of egg have formed ribbons of omelette. Remove from the oil with a slotted spoon, drain on paper towels and keep warm. (If preferred, make a 1-egg omelette and cut into strips.)

In a wok, heat the remaining oil and stir-fry the shallots and garlic until golden brown. Remove from the wok with a slotted spoon, drain on paper towels and keep warm.

Add the prawns and sliced chicken to the oil remaining in the wok and stir-fry for 5 minutes. Drain the excess oil from the wok and stir in the tamarind juice, sugar, tao chiew and nam pla. Cook for 5 minutes or until the mixture becomes sticky.

Reduce the heat to very low and return the vermicelli, fried shallots and garlic to the pan. Mix gently but thoroughly and allow the mixture to warm through for 2 to 3 minutes.

Transfer to a large shallow serving dish, top with the fried omelette strips and garnish with pickled garlic, sliced red chilli and coriander leaves.

Left: Soft Rice Vermicelli in Coconut Milk; right: Crispy Sweet and Sour Rice Vermicelli

Soft Rice Vermicelli in Coconut Milk

Meeh Ka Ti

225 g (8 oz) soaked rice vermicelli
2 teaspoons oil
2 eggs, beaten
500 ml (18 fl oz) coconut milk (see page 63)
6 shallots, or ½ onion, roughly chopped
225 g (8 oz) raw prawns, shelled and deveined (page 63)
4 tablespoons tao chiew (salted soya bean flavouring)
2 tablespoons sugar
2 tablespoons tamarind juice (see page 62) or 1 tablespoon lemon juice
300 g (11 oz) bean sprouts
100 g (4 oz) gui chai leaves or spring onion tops

To garnish:
3 tablespoons chopped coriander leaves
2 red chillies, seeded and sliced
1 lemon, sliced lengthways

Bring a large saucepan of water to the boil, add the vermicelli and cook, stirring occasionally, for 15 minutes. Drain and set aside.

Heat the oil in an omelette pan or frying pan and add the eggs. Tilt the pan to form an omelette, lifting the sides of the omelette to allow any uncooked egg mixture to flow underneath. When the omelette is cooked, remove it from the pan and slice into thin shreds. Keep warm until required.

In a large saucepan or wok, bring the coconut milk to the boil. Cook over medium to high heat for 10 minutes or until a film of oil forms on the top. Stir in the shallots, prawns, tao chiew, sugar, tamarind juice or lemon juice. Mix well and cook for 5 minutes. Transfer half the mixture to a bowl and keep warm for the topping.

To the remainder of the mixture in the saucepan, add the reserved vermicelli. Mix well and cook for 5 minutes. Stir in half the bean sprouts and gui chai leaves, mixing thoroughly.

Pile the vermicelli mixture on to a shallow serving dish, top with the reserved prawn mixture and garnish with coriander, chilli and lemon slices. Serve with remaining bean sprouts and gui chai leaves.

Variation: Sliced chicken breast or pork fillet may be used instead of prawns, or a combination of meat and shellfish.

Salads & Vegetables

These eight pages contain some of the book's most exciting recipes. Thailand, like other hot countries the world over, has a large salad repertoire: one could enjoy summer meal after summer meal based on the recipes that follow. And regular diners at Thai restaurants will be delighted to find recipes for four piquant dipping sauces, those ever-popular adjuncts to fried and deep-fried foods.

48

Prawn Salad with Lemon Grass

Plah Gung

*275 g (10 oz) raw prawns, shelled and deveined
(see page 63)
4 tablespoons water
200 g (7 oz) onions, finely sliced
5 small Thai chillies, crushed, or ½ teaspoon ground
chilli
3 tablespoons finely chopped fresh basil or mint
leaves
3 tablespoons finely chopped takrai (lemon grass)
3 tablespoons lemon juice
3 tablespoons nam pla (fish gravy)
½ teaspoon sugar*

*To garnish:
1 lettuce, separated into leaves
1 tablespoon chopped coriander leaves*

In Thailand, it is usual to serve three or four salads at a snack meal, with a selection of dipping sauces.

Place the prawns in a large shallow saucepan with the water and cook over moderate heat until the prawns turn pink. Do not boil, or the prawns will become tough.

Meanwhile, combine the onions, chillies, basil leaves, takrai, lemon juice, nam pla and sugar in a bowl and mix well. With a slotted spoon, transfer the prawns to the bowl and stir very gently.

Arrange a bed of lettuce on a shallow serving dish. Top with the prawn mixture and garnish with coriander.

Squid Salad

Yum Pla Mhouk

*300 g (11 oz) squid, cleaned (see page 63)
1 medium onion, quartered and sliced
3 small Thai chillies, finely chopped, or 1 teaspoon
ground chilli
3 sprigs fresh mint, leaves chopped
1½ tablespoons lemon juice
1 tablespoon nam pla (fish gravy)
½ teaspoon sugar*

*To garnish:
1 lettuce, separated into leaves
3 tablespoons chopped coriander leaves*

Slice the prepared squid into neat slices or rounds. Place it in a saucepan and cook, stirring constantly, for 5 minutes. Remove from the heat and allow to cool.

With a slotted spoon, transfer the squid to a bowl and stir in the remaining ingredients, except the garnish.

Arrange a bed of lettuce on a shallow serving dish, top with the squid mixture and garnish with coriander. Serve immediately.

Top left: Prawn Salad with Lemon Grass; bottom right: Squid Salad

Beef and Galanga Salad

Larb Nua

2 tablespoons glutinous rice
300 g (11 oz) minced beef
5 slices galanga (khar root), sliced
3 tablespoons chopped spring onion
1 teaspoon ground chilli, or to taste
3–4 tablespoons lemon juice
3 tablespoons nam pla (fish gravy)
½ teaspoon sugar
4–5 sprigs mint, leaves chopped
3 tablespoons chopped shallots

To garnish:
1 lettuce, separated into leaves

Place the glutinous rice in a saucepan over moderate heat and dry-fry, stirring constantly, for 10 minutes, or until the grains are light brown in colour. Remove from the heat. Grind in a blender or food processor, or pound in a mortar with a pestle until very fine.

Put the minced beef into a saucepan over gentle heat and cook for 10 to 15 minutes, stirring constantly, until the meat is cooked and all the liquid has been absorbed. Transfer to a mixing bowl and stir in the ground rice. Add all the remaining ingredients, except the garnish, and mix well.

Arrange a bed of lettuce on a shallow serving dish, and top with the beef mixture. Serve immediately. Side dishes of shredded cabbage, green beans, spring onions and fresh basil leaves may be served as accompaniments.

Variation: Minced chicken or pork may be used instead of beef.

Left: North-eastern Beef Salad with a selection of raw vegetables; right: Beef and Bamboo Shoot Salad

Beef and Bamboo Shoot Salad

Yum Nua Noh Mai

200 g (7 oz) fillet or rump steak, thinly sliced
200 ml (⅓ pint) coconut cream or milk
2 × 100 g (4 oz) pieces bamboo shoot, sliced
1½ tablespoons cooked red curry paste
(see page 63)
2 tablespoons chopped takrai (lemon grass)
1½ teaspoons finely chopped makrut (citrus) leaves
2 tablespoons lemon juice
1½ teaspoons nam pla (fish gravy)
3 small Thai chillies or ½ teaspoon ground chilli

To garnish:
1 lettuce, separated into leaves
½ tablespoon shredded red chilli

Place the beef in a small saucepan with the coconut cream and cook over low heat for 10 to 15 minutes or until the beef is tender and has absorbed most of the coconut cream. (Any liquid remaining in the pan should have an oily appearance.) Remove the pan from the heat and set aside until the meat is cool.

Transfer the beef to a bowl. Add the remaining ingredients, except the garnish, and mix well.

Arrange a bed of lettuce on a shallow serving dish, top with the beef mixture and garnish with the chilli. Serve immediately.

North-Eastern Beef Salad

Nua Nam Tok

2 tablespoons glutinous rice
300 g (11 oz) rump steak
4 tablespoons water
2 medium onions, finely chopped
3 tablespoons fresh mint leaves, chopped
1 teaspoon ground chilli, or to taste
2 tablespoons lemon juice
2 tablespoons nam pla (fish gravy)
½ teaspoon sugar

To garnish:
1 lettuce, separated into leaves
2 tablespoons chopped coriander leaves

Charcoal-grilled steak is best for this delicious salad. However, conventionally grilled meat may be used with excellent results. In North-Eastern Thailand, where glutinous rice is a staple food, this salad is a popular (and very hot) dish. Adjust the quantity of ground chilli to taste.

Place the glutinous rice in a saucepan over moderate heat and dry-fry, stirring constantly, for 10 minutes, or until the grains are light brown in colour. Remove from the heat. Grind in a blender or food processor, or pound in a mortar with a pestle, until very fine.

Place the steak under a preheated grill and cook under high heat for 2 minutes on each side, then reduce the heat and cook for a further 4 to 6 minutes or until medium cooked. Set aside until cool.

Slice the steak and place in a saucepan with the water. Cook over high heat for 1 minute, stirring constantly.

Remove the pan from the heat and stir in the ground rice, onions, mint, ground chilli, lemon juice, nam pla and sugar.

Arrange a bed of lettuce on a shallow serving dish, top with the beef mixture and garnish with the chopped coriander leaves.

Serve immediately, with a selection of chopped vegetables, such as blanched green beans, cabbage, spring onions and carrots.
Variation: Liver may be substituted for the steak. Ox liver is traditionally used, but lamb's liver is equally successful.

Thai Sweet and Sour Salad

Som Tum

1 large clove garlic, chopped
2 small Thai chillies, chopped, or ½ teaspoon ground chilli
100 g (4 oz) carrots, shredded
100 g (4 oz) white cabbage, shredded
2 green beans, cut in 2.5 cm (1 inch) lengths
2 tomatoes, chopped
1½ tablespoons nam pla (fish gravy)
3 tablespoons lemon juice
3 tablespoons sugar
1 tablespoon ground dried shrimp
2 tablespoons crushed roasted peanuts
1 lettuce, separated into leaves, to garnish

In North-Eastern Thailand, where this dish originated, it would be made with green papayas. A combination of carrots and cabbage works just as well, however. Serve the salad with Grilled Chicken (see page 30) and steamed glutinous rice.

Grind the garlic and the chillies in a blender or food processor, or pound in a mortar with a pestle.

Transfer the mixture to a mixing bowl, add all the remaining ingredients except the lettuce, and mix well so that all the ingredients are thoroughly blended.

Arrange a bed of lettuce on a shallow serving dish, top with the salad, and serve immediately.

Fried Mixed Vegetables

Bhud Bhug Raum Mid

3 tablespoons vegetable oil
1 clove garlic, crushed
100 g (4 oz) cabbage, shredded
100 g (4 oz) cauliflower florets
½ teaspoon freshly ground black pepper
2 tablespoons oyster sauce
150 ml (¼ pint) chicken or vegetable stock
100 g (4 oz) broccoli, trimmed and sliced
2 carrots, scraped and cut in matchstick lengths
100 g (4 oz) button mushrooms, wiped and sliced
1 onion, sliced
50 g (2 oz) bean sprouts (optional)

Heat the oil in a wok. Add the garlic and stir-fry until golden brown. Add the cabbage and cauliflower, with the pepper. Stir in the oyster sauce and stock and cook, stirring constantly, for 3 minutes.

Add the broccoli, carrots, mushrooms, onion and bean sprouts, if using. Stir-fry for 2 minutes more. Transfer to a large dish or platter and serve immediately. **Note:** Vary the vegetables according to what is in season. Courgettes and green beans are tasty additions; so are yellow, red and green peppers.

Fried Aubergine with Soya Bean Flavouring

Ma Khoa Bhud Tao Chiew

2 tablespoons oil
1 clove garlic, crushed
1 medium aubergine, cut into 2.5 cm (1 inch) cubes
2 tablespoons water
1 tablespoon tao chiew (salted soya bean flavouring)
1 teaspoon dark soy sauce
1 tablespoon sugar
½ teaspoon freshly ground black pepper
3 tablespoons sweet basil leaves
1 red chilli, seeded and finely chopped

Heat the oil in a wok or large frying pan, add the garlic and stir-fry for 1 minute or until golden.

Push the garlic to one side of the pan, add the aubergine cubes and stir-fry for 5 minutes, or until cooked, adding the water as necessary to prevent the aubergine from sticking to the pan.

Stir in the tao chiew, dark soy sauce, sugar and pepper and heat through, stirring, for 1 to 2 minutes.

Finally add the basil and chilli and mix thoroughly. Spoon the mixture on to a serving dish and serve at once.

White Cabbage Salad

Yum Kra Khum Plee

300 g (11 oz) white cabbage, shredded
3 tablespoons vegetable oil
1 tablespoon sliced shallots
1 clove garlic, crushed
1 tablespoon chopped dried red chillies
1 teaspoon salt
1 tablespoon nam pla (fish gravy)
1½ tablespoons lemon juice
1 tablespoon crushed roasted peanuts
4 tablespoons coconut cream
10 cooked prawns, shelled, deveined and halved lengthways (see page 63)
225 g (8 oz) sliced roast pork

Place the cabbage in a saucepan, add boiling water to cover and cook over high heat for 2 minutes. Drain the cabbage in a colander, refresh under cold water and drain again. Heat the oil in a frying pan. Add the shallots and stir-fry for 2 minutes. With a slotted spoon, transfer the shallots to paper towels to drain.

Add the garlic to the oil remaining in the frying pan and fry over gentle heat until golden. Drain as for the shallots. Cook and drain the red chillies in the same way, adding more oil if necessary.

Transfer the cabbage to a large bowl. Add the salt, nam pla, lemon juice, peanuts, coconut cream, prawns and sliced pork. Mix well. Spoon the salad on to a large platter, sprinkle with the shallots, garlic and chillies and serve immediately.

Vermicelli Salad

Yum Wun Sen

660 ml (1 pint plus 4 tablespoons) water
100 g (4 oz) vermicelli, soaked in boiling water until soft, then cut in 1 cm (½ inch) lengths
100 g (4 oz) minced pork
100 g (4 oz) raw prawns, shelled, deveined and halved lengthways (see page 63)
2 tablespoons vegetable oil
2 tablespoons dried shrimp
2 cloves garlic, crushed
4 tablespoons nam pla (fish gravy)
4 tablespoons lemon juice
1 teaspoon sugar
5 small Thai chillies or 1 teaspoon ground chilli
1 onion, finely chopped
2 sticks celery, finely sliced

To garnish:
1 lettuce, separated into leaves
2 tablespoons chopped coriander leaves

Bring 600 ml (1 pint) of the water to the boil in a medium saucepan.

Add the vermicelli and cook for 3 minutes. Drain in a colander, then rinse gently but thoroughly under cold

Top left: White Cabbage Salad; bottom right: Fried Mixed Vegetables

water. Drain again and transfer the vermicelli to a mixing bowl.

Place the minced pork in a saucepan with the prawns and remaining water and cook, stirring constantly, for 5 to 7 minutes or until the pork is cooked through.

Remove the pork from the heat and allow to cool while you cook the remaining ingredients.

Heat the oil in a saucepan, add the dried shrimp and stir-fry over moderate heat for 5 minutes. With a slotted spoon, transfer the shrimp to paper towels and set aside.

Add the garlic to the oil remaining in the pan and fry until golden, then pour the oil and garlic over the vermicelli. Add the pork and prawn mixture, the nam pla, lemon juice, sugar, chillies, onion and celery and mix well.

Arrange a bed of lettuce on a shallow serving dish. Top with the vermicelli mixture and sprinkle with dried shrimp. Garnish with coriander.

Serve immediately.

Cucumber Salad

Ah Jard

3 tablespoons white vinegar
3 tablespoons white sugar
¼ teaspoon salt
½ medium cucumber, quartered and sliced
¼ medium onion, chopped, or 4 shallots, sliced

To garnish (optional):
shredded red chilli
coriander leaves

In a saucepan, mix together the vinegar, sugar and salt, and boil until clear. Remove from the heat and allow to cool.

Place the sliced cucumber in a serving dish, and arrange the onion or shallots on top. Just before serving, pour over the dressing.

Soya Bean Dipping Sauce

Tow Jiew Lhon

450 ml (¾ pint) coconut milk
4 shallots, sliced
4 tablespoons tao chiew (salted soya bean
flavouring)
3 tablespoons raw prawns, shelled, deveined and
finely chopped (see page 63)
3 tablespoons minced pork
3 red chillies
3 tablespoons sugar
3 tablespoons tamarind juice (see page 62)
salt (optional)

This sauce is an alternative to *nam prig* and may be used in any of the ways suggested in the previous recipe.

Bring the coconut milk to the boil in a saucepan. Lower the heat and simmer for 10 minutes.

Meanwhile, place half the shallots in a mortar with the tao chiew and grind to a paste with a pestle. Add the shallot paste to the coconut milk with the prawns, minced pork and whole chillies.

Cook over gentle heat, stirring constantly, for 5 minutes, then stir in the remaining shallots, sugar and tamarind juice. Taste and add salt if necessary.

Shrimp Dipping Sauce

Kapee Khua

3 dried red chillies, seeded and soaked in boiling
water until soft
2 tablespoons chopped takrai (lemon grass)
6 shallots, finely chopped
3 tablespoons chopped krachai root
3 tablespoons kapee (shrimp paste)
50 g (2 oz) dried shrimp or ground dried fish
300 ml (½ pint) coconut milk
100 g (4 oz) minced pork
4 red chillies
3 tablespoons palm sugar or demerara
3 tablespoons nam pla (fish gravy)

Grind the dried red chillies, takrai, shallots, krachai root and shrimp paste in a blender or food processor, or pound in a mortar with a pestle. When the mixture forms a paste, add the dried shrimp or fish and grind again.

Bring the coconut milk to the boil in a saucepan, lower the heat and cook for 10 minutes or until a film of oil forms on the top. Add the ground chilli mixture and cook, stirring constantly, for 5 minutes.

Add the minced pork and whole chillies and cook, stirring, for 10 minutes. Finally stir in the palm sugar and nam pla.

Serve with fried fish, prawns or vegetables.

Anchovy and Coconut Milk Dipping Sauce with Fish

Pla Rah Lhon

175 g (6 oz) pla rah (Thai anchovies – see Note)
3 tablespoons water
450 ml (¾ pint) coconut milk (see page 63)
10 shallots or 1 medium onion, chopped
2 tablespoons finely chopped krachai root
1 tablespoon finely chopped galanga (khar root)
2 tablespoons finely chopped takrai (lemon grass)
2 makrut (citrus) leaves, torn into shreds
3 red chillies
225 g (8 oz) cod fillet, in 4 pieces
2 × 100 g (4 oz) pieces bamboo shoot, sliced
3 small green aubergines, sliced
5 green beans, cut in 2.5 cm (1 inch) lengths

Place the anchovies in a saucepan with the water and bring to the boil.

Lower the heat and simmer for 10 minutes or until the anchovy flesh breaks down to a paste. Remove any bones that have not dissolved.

Add the coconut milk to the anchovies in the pan and bring to the boil, stirring.

Add the shallots, krachai root, galanga (khar root), takrai, makrut leaves and whole chillies. Stir well and allow the mixture to return to the boil.

Lower the heat, add the fish to the pan and cook for 5 minutes, then stir in the bamboo shoots, aubergines and beans.

Cook for 5 minutes more, stirring the mixture occasionally.

Taste the sauce and add salt if necessary.

Transfer the dipping sauce to a serving bowl and serve with a selection of fresh vegetables.

Note: For this recipe you will need about three quarters of a small (227 g/8 oz) jar of Thai anchovies. Drain the anchovies thoroughly before use.

Shrimp Paste Sauce

Nam Prig Bhug

3 small cloves garlic, chopped
5 small Thai chillies, chopped
1 tablespoon kapee (shrimp paste)
2 tablespoons lemon juice
1 tablespoon palm sugar or demerara
½ teaspoon nam pla (fish gravy)
1 teaspoon ground dried shrimp

Nam prig is a universal Thai sauce. It is usually served with a selection of vegetables, either raw or boiled or deep-fried in batter, but equally often accompanies omelettes, fried fish, smoked mackerel or prawns. It is particularly good with slices of aubergine, dipped in beaten egg and fried in hot oil until golden brown.

Grind or pound the garlic and chillies together. Transfer to a small bowl and add all the remaining ingredients. Mix well and use as suggested above.

Shrimp Paste Sauce with accompaniments

55

Desserts

Thai desserts merit more attention than they are customarily given. The recipes are often very inventive: prawns, mung beans and seaweed may not, to Western ways of thinking, be the ideal raw ingredients for a rich, sticky dessert, but, once you have tried them, you'll see how delicious they can be.
It may take a little practice to perfect the culinary skills needed to make these desserts, but an attractive feature of the recipes is their flexibility: many can be made in advance, when you have more time to prepare them.

56

Coconut Milk Custard

Sung Kha Yha

6 eggs
250 ml (8 fl oz) coconut milk (see page 63)
175 g (6 oz) palm sugar or demerara
100 g (4 oz) white sugar
1 teaspoon vanilla essence

In Thailand, custards are often baked in natural containers like hollowed-out young coconuts or the shells of small pumpkins. Small heat-resistant bowls may be used equally successfully, however.

Combine all the ingredients in a mixing bowl and beat well with a hand-held electric mixer or wire whisk.

Divide the mixture between 4 coconut shells or 2 pumpkin shells, or use 4 heat-resistant bowls of approximately 250 ml (8 fl oz) capacity. Place the shells or bowls in the top of one or two steamers, packing them closely together and keeping them upright with crumpled greaseproof paper if necessary.

Place over boiling water and steam for 30 minutes. Test one of the custards with the tip of a sharp knife. If it comes out clean, the custard is cooked. Serve warm or cold.

Variation: To add texture to the custards, shredded young coconut, pumpkin seeds or lotus seeds may be stirred into the basic mixture before steaming.

Taro Balls in Coconut Milk

Kha Nom Bua Loy

500 g (1 lb) taro roots
175 g (6 oz) arrowroot
about 2 litres (3½ pints) water
120 ml (4 fl oz) coconut milk (see page 63)
175 g (6 oz) sugar
2 tablespoons palm sugar or demerara
½ teaspoon salt

Clean the taro roots thoroughly, cut them in half and place in the top of a steamer. Place over boiling water and steam for 30 to 40 minutes or until the centre of each root is soft. Remove from the steamer and set the roots aside. When cool enough to handle, mash or grate the cooked taro and reserve until required.

Place 4 tablespoons of the arrowroot in a bowl and add 2 tablespoons water. Mix to a paste, then gradually add 120 ml (4 fl oz) boiling water, stirring constantly. A clear sauce should be formed. If the mixture is still cloudy, transfer it to a saucepan and cook over low heat, stirring constantly, until it clears.

Pour the arrowroot sauce into a mixing bowl, add the mashed taro and mix well. Stir in the remaining arrowroot and mix to a firm dough, adding extra arrowroot if required. (The amount of moisture in the taro will determine how much arrowroot is needed.)

Roll the taro dough into little balls, each about 1 cm

Mung Bean Balls in Syrup

(½ inch) in diameter. Place on a tray and set aside.

Bring the remaining 1.75 litres (3 pints) of water to the boil in a large saucepan. In a second saucepan combine the coconut milk, sugar, palm sugar and salt. Bring to the boil.

To cook the taro balls, lower them carefully, in batches, into the boiling water. When they float to the surface, remove them with a slotted spoon and add them to the coconut milk mixture. Allow the sweetened coconut milk to return to the boil, then remove the pan from the heat and transfer the coconut balls with the sweetened coconut milk to a serving bowl. Serve warm or cold.

Mung Bean Balls in Syrup

Med Kha Nhoon

175 g (6 oz) shelled split mung beans
2 litres (3½ pints) water
250 ml (8 fl oz) coconut milk
925 g (1 lb 14 oz) sugar
1 teaspoon vanilla essence
20 egg yolks

Wash the beans under cold water three or four times, or until the water runs clear.

Transfer the beans to a large saucepan, add 1.2 litres (2 pints) water and bring to the boil. Lower the heat and simmer for 20 minutes, then drain the beans thoroughly and return them to the clean saucepan with the coconut milk and 175 g (6 oz) sugar.

Cook over low heat, stirring constantly with a wooden spoon, until the mixture thickens and forms a dry mixture capable of being shaped. To test if the mixture is of the correct consistency, remove it from the heat, cool slightly, then prod gently with a clean finger. If the mixture does not stick to the finger it is ready. Beat in the vanilla essence and allow the mixture to cool completely.

When the bean mixture is quite cold, form it into small oval shapes, about 2.5 cm (1 inch) long and 1 cm (½ inch) wide. Arrange on a tray and set aside.

Place the remaining water in a large saucepan with the remaining sugar and bring to the boil, stirring constantly, until all the sugar has dissolved. Boil, without stirring, for 5 minutes.

Meanwhile beat the egg yolks lightly in a shallow bowl.

Remove the sugar syrup from the heat. Dip the mung bean balls in the egg yolk, then add them to the pan of syrup. When the surface of the syrup is covered with coated mung bean balls, return the pan to the heat and bring the syrup to the boil. Boil for 5 minutes, turning the bean balls over halfway through cooking. When all the bean balls are cooked, transfer them to a serving dish with a slotted spoon.

Repeat the dipping and cooking process until all the bean balls are cooked. Serve hot or cold.

Sticky Rice with Coconut Milk

Khow-Nheaw Moon

500 g (1 lb) glutinous rice
400 ml (14 fl oz) coconut milk
175 g (6 oz) sugar
1 tablespoon salt

Sticky rice pudding is very popular in Thailand. The prawn topping (recipe follows) is a favourite semi-savoury accompaniment. The less adventurous might prefer to try it with mangoes or other tropical fruit, or with Coconut Milk Custard (page 56).

Before using the glutinous rice, wash it thoroughly and soak in water to cover for at least 3 hours, preferably overnight.

Next day, drain the rice thoroughly and spread it out in the top of a large steamer. Place the steamer over boiling water and steam for 30 to 40 minutes or until the rice is cooked.

Meanwhile combine the coconut milk, sugar and salt in a saucepan and bring to the boil over moderate heat, stirring constantly. When the mixture boils, stir in the rice, remove from the heat, cover and allow to stand for 15 minutes. Serve with Prawn Topping (below) or as suggested above.

58

Prawn Topping

Nah Gung

175 g (6 oz) raw prawns, shelled, deveined and
minced (see page 63)
100 g (4 oz) shredded coconut
½ teaspoon ground turmeric
3 tablespoons oil
1 teaspoon finely chopped coriander root or stem
1 teaspoon freshly ground black pepper
2 teaspoons salt
2 tablespoons sugar
1 tablespoon finely shredded makrut (citrus) leaves
or coriander leaves, to decorate

This unusual topping is traditionally served in Thailand as an accompaniment to the dessert in the previous recipe.

In a small bowl, mix the prawns with the coconut and ground turmeric. Set aside.

Heat the oil in a frying pan and stir-fry the coriander root and pepper for 2 minutes.

Add the minced prawn mixture with the salt and sugar and cook for a further 5 minutes, stirring occasionally.

Spoon the mixture over the sticky rice pudding, decorate with makrut or coriander leaves and serve.

Golden Threads in Syrup

Phoy Tong

1 egg
11 egg yolks
500 ml (18 fl oz) water
750 g (1½ lb) sugar

To make this delicious dessert you will need 4 grease-proof paper cones, of the type used for piping cream or icing.

Mix the whole egg and egg yolks in a large mixing bowl. Beat with a hand-held electric mixer or a wire whisk until frothy, then strain into a large jug.

Combine the water and sugar in a large saucepan and bring to the boil, stirring until all the sugar has dissolved. Boil steadily, without stirring, for 5 minutes, then make the golden threads. Grasp a paper cone firmly in the right hand (with a fingertip blocking the nozzle) and fill the cone with egg mixture. Hold it over the boiling syrup, release the finger and drizzle the egg mixture into the syrup, using a spiral movement in one direction only. Try not to break the thread before the cone is empty. As soon as the threads are cooked – and they cook very quickly – remove them from the syrup, using chopsticks or a fork. Drain on crumpled paper towels.

Add a little water if the syrup has become too thick and repeat the process with the remaining cones.

Serve the golden threads piled on a decorative dish.

Seaweed Jelly with Custard Topping

Wun Sang Kha Yha

10 g (¼ oz) soaked seaweed jelly
500 ml (18 fl oz) water
500 g (1 lb) sugar
flavouring (see Note)

Custard topping:
10 g (¼ oz) soaked seaweed jelly
750 ml (1¼ pints) water
100 g (4 oz) white sugar
250 ml (8 fl oz) coconut milk
75 g (3 oz) palm sugar or demerara
3 eggs
1 teaspoon vanilla essence

To make the jelly base, mix the seaweed jelly, water and sugar in a saucepan. Bring to the boil, stirring until all the sugar has dissolved, then add colouring or flavouring, if liked, and pour into a 28 × 18 cm (11 × 7 inch) Swiss roll tin. Set aside to cool and then refrigerate until firm.

When the base has set, prepare the topping. Combine the jelly, water and white sugar in a saucepan. Bring to the boil, stirring until the sugar has dissolved.

Meanwhile, in a second pan, heat the coconut milk with the palm sugar, stirring until the palm sugar has dissolved.

Beat the eggs in a bowl, add about 4 tablespoons of the hot coconut milk mixture, beating thoroughly, then return the egg mixture to the coconut milk mixture in the pan and mix thoroughly.

Remove the egg and coconut milk mixture from the heat and pour it into the saucepan containing the jelly, beating constantly. Stir in the vanilla essence and bring the mixture to the boil, stirring until it thickens.

Allow to cool, then carefully pour the mixture on top of the chilled jelly layer in the Swiss roll tin. Refrigerate until set, then cut out squares or triangles or use biscuit cutters to make fancy shapes.

Serve on a large platter.

Note: Edible food colouring may be added to the jelly, or it may be flavoured with chopped water chestnuts or golden threads (see page 58). At Easter time serve it in eggshells for a special children's treat.

Left: Golden Threads in Syrup; right: Seaweed Jelly with Custard Topping

Top right: Bananas in Syrup, Sala Thai Style; bottom left: Coconut-topped Pudding

Coconut-Topped Pudding

Ta-Kho

75 g (3 oz) rice flour
2 tablespoons cornflour
250 ml (8 fl oz) water
1 tablespoon soft brown sugar
225 g (8 oz) white sugar
50 g (2 oz) water chestnuts, finely chopped, or 25 g
(1 oz) lotus seeds

Topping:
350 ml (12 fl oz) coconut milk
1 tablespoon rice flour
1½ tablespoons cornflour
1 teaspoon salt
rose petals, theoy leaves or golden threads, to
decorate

To make the base, combine the rice flour, cornflour and water in a mixing bowl. Mix well, then strain into a saucepan. Stir in the sugars, mixing well. Set the pan over moderate heat and bring to the boil, stirring constantly, then lower the heat and cook, stirring, for 5 minutes more. Stir in the water chestnuts or lotus seeds. Divide the mixture between 6 small bowls, filling them about one third full. Set aside to cool.

Meanwhile make the topping by combining all the ingredients, except the decoration, in a medium saucepan. Place over low heat and cook, stirring constantly, for about 10 minutes until the mixture forms a thick custard. Allow to cool slightly, then spoon the topping carefully on top of the rice flour layer in each bowl.

Set the bowls aside until the custards are quite cold, then decorate with rose petals, theoy leaves or golden threads (see page 58).

Bananas in Syrup, Sala Thai Style

Sala Thai Gluy Chium

500 ml (18 fl oz) water
500 g (1 lb) sugar
6 large bananas (not too ripe), peeled and quartered
2 tablespoons rum
10 fl oz (½ pint) single cream

Most Thai desserts take a long time (and considerable effort) to prepare. Here is a simple sweet adapted to Western tastes which can be made in under half an hour.

Bring the water and sugar to the boil in a large saucepan, stirring constantly until all the sugar has dissolved. Boil for 5 minutes without stirring.

Lower the heat, add the bananas and cook for 10 to 15 minutes or until all the bananas feel soft when tested with a wooden skewer.

Add the rum, stirring gently so as not to break up the bananas, and cook over very low heat for 5 minutes

more. Carefully transfer the bananas to a shallow serving dish, ladle over a little of the syrup and serve warm or cold with cream.

Theoy Balls with Mung Bean Filling

Theoy Pab

100 g (4 oz) mung beans, picked over and washed
2 tablespoons sugar
½ teaspoon salt
2 tablespoons roasted sesame seeds
175 g (6 oz) fresh coconut, shredded
a handful of theoy leaves
175 g (6 oz) glutinous rice flour
120 ml (4 fl oz) water
1–2 tablespoons plain sesame seeds

This dessert is best made with fresh coconut, shredded just before use. If the coconut must be prepared in advance it should be steamed for 5 minutes after shredding.

Soak the mung beans in cold water to cover for 6 to 8 hours, preferably overnight.

Next day, drain the beans and spread them out in the top of a steamer. Set over boiling water and steam for 30 to 40 minutes until soft.

Transfer the beans to a bowl, mash thoroughly and stir in ¼ teaspoon of the sugar, ¼ teaspoon of the salt and all the roasted sesame seeds. Reserve.

Combine the shredded coconut with the remaining salt and spread out on a shallow tray.

Bring a medium saucepan of water to the boil, add the theoy leaves and cook for 2 minutes to extract the colour. Remove the leaves with a slotted spoon but retain the coloured liquid.

Combine the glutinous rice flour and measured water to form a dough, adding enough of the theoy liquid to colour the dough. Reserve the remaining theoy liquid in the pan.

Divide the dough into small balls, about 2.5 cm (1 inch) in diameter, and flatten them lightly.

Return the saucepan of theoy liquid to the stove and bring to the boil. Add the dough balls, a few at a time, so that the liquid continues to boil. When the balls float on the surface, they are done. Remove with a slotted spoon and place on the coconut-coated tray to cool.

As soon as the balls are cool enough to handle, make a hole in each of them with a clean wooden spoon handle or thumb. Place a little of the mung bean filling in each hole, squeeze the edges together to enclose the filling and roll the balls in shredded coconut.

Arrange on a serving plate, sprinkle with the remaining sugar and plain sesame seeds, and serve.

61

Foundation Recipes

Many different sauces and mixes are fundamental ingredients in Thai cooking. Some are available commercially, but home-made versions have the best flavour. The following are those which occur frequently in this book.

Garlic Mixture

Kra Tium-Prig Tai

2 tablespoons crushed garlic
2 tablespoons chopped coriander root or stem
½ tablespoon ground black pepper

This simple mixture is an essential ingredient in many Thai dishes. Pound all the ingredients together in a mortar with a pestle until they are thoroughly blended and form a paste. Use as required. For the strongest flavour, the mixture is best made up when needed, but it can be made in advance, if liked, and stored, covered, in the refrigerator for a day or two.

Tempura Batter

Pang Tempura

1 egg
150 ml (¼ pint) cold water
100 g (4 oz) self-raising flour
2 tablespoons cornflour
1 teaspoon baking powder

In a bowl, mix together the egg and water. Sift in the flour, cornflour and baking powder and mix in quickly with a fork or a pair of chopsticks. Do not overmix: the batter should still be slightly lumpy. Use as required.

Plum Sauce

Num Beuy

3 preserved plums, with 1 tablespoon liquid from the jar
150 ml (¼ pint) water
6 tablespoons white sugar

In a saucepan, mix the plum liquid and the water and add the plums. Boil for 1 to 2 minutes, stirring con-

stantly with a wooden spoon to break up the plum flesh. Press the mixture through a sieve, and return to the saucepan.

Add the sugar, bring to the boil, reduce the heat and simmer for 15 minutes, until the sauce thickens and is reddish in colour. Cover and store in a cool place.

Tamarind Juice

Num Som Ma Kharm

25 g (1 oz) tamarind
5 fl oz (¼ pint) warm water

Wash the tamarind and leave it to soak in the water for 5 to 10 minutes (the longer the tamarind is left to soak, the stronger the flavour). Squeeze out as much tamarind pulp as possible, then press the thickened liquid through a sieve, and use as required.

If the tamarind juice is to be stored, it should be sieved into a saucepan and brought to the boil, then allowed to cool before covering and storing in a cool place.

Tamarind Sauce

Num Som Ma Kharm (Prung)

5 fl oz (¼ pint) tamarind juice
100 g (4 oz) demerara sugar
2 tablespoons nam pla (fish gravy)

A simple tamarind sauce can be made with the above ingredients. Add the sugar and nam pla to the tamarind juice, bring to the boil and simmer, stirring occasionally, until the sugar is dissolved and the sauce is thick.

Red Curry Paste

Kang Bhed Dang

6 dried red chillies, seeded, soaked and roughly chopped
2 tablespoons chopped takri (lemon grass)
1 teaspoon chopped coriander root or stem
1 tablespoon chopped shallots
1 tablespoon chopped garlic
1 teaspoon chopped galanga (khar root)
2 teaspoons coriander seeds
1 teaspoon cumin seeds
6 white peppercorns
1 teaspoon salt
1 teaspoon shrimp paste

Grind all the ingredients in a blender or food processor, or pound to a paste in a mortar with a pestle.
Variations:
1 For green curry paste, substitute 20 small Thai chillies (prig khie nhou) for the red chillies.
2 Makrut, a strongly flavoured citrus fruit, makes a good addition to this curry paste. Reduce the amount of takrai to 1 tablespoon and add ½ tablespoon chopped makrut rind. Do not add the coriander or cumin seeds to this variation.
3 Dried shrimp may also be added for a slightly different flavour. Add 2 tablespoons to the makrut variation above, with the shrimp paste.

Cooked Red Curry Paste

Nam Prig Bhao

5 shallots
5 garlic cloves
1 tablespoon kapee (shrimp paste)
150 ml (¼ pint) vegetable oil
5 dried red chillies, seeded
1 tablespoon palm sugar or demerara
1 tablespoon nam pla (fish gravy)
1 teaspoon tamarind juice (see page 62)
1 tablespoon ground shrimp

Wrap the shrimp paste in foil and place under a pre-heated grill with the shallots and garlic cloves for 5 minutes, turning half way through grilling.

Heat the oil in a small frying pan or wok and stir-fry the dried chillies over a medium heat for ½ minute. Do not discard the oil. Unwrap the shrimp paste, peel the shallots and garlic cloves and place in a mortar or food processor. Add the chillies and blend to a thin paste.

Return the paste to the oil in the frying pan and add the sugar, nam pla, tamarind juice and ground shrimp. Stir-fry over a medium heat for 5 minutes and leave to cool.

Use to flavour prawn crackers, as a snack spread on toast or as a spicy flavouring for salads or soups. The paste may also be used in cooking to baste pork crackling. Stored in an air-tight jar in the refrigerator, it will keep for several weeks.

Paprika Oil

Num Mun Prig

4 tablespoons vegetable, sunflower or soya oil
1 tablespoon ground paprika

Heat the oil in a small frying pan. Add the ground paprika and cook over gentle heat for 1 minute, stirring to ensure that the oil and paprika are well blended.

Garlic Oil

Num Mun Kra Tium

4 tablespoons vegetable, sunflower or soya oil
1 tablespoon crushed garlic

Heat the oil in a small frying pan and add the crushed garlic. Cook over gentle heat until the garlic is golden, stirring occasionally, and use as required.

Coconut cream

Kati Gon

400 g (14 oz) grated or dessicated coconut
900 ml (1½ pints) milk

Combine the coconut and milk in a saucepan, bring to the boil, lower the heat and simmer, stirring occasionally, until the mixture is reduced by one third. Strain, pressing the mixture against the sides of the strainer to extract as much liquid as possible, then pour the coconut milk into a bowl and chill in the refrigerator. When quite cold, skim off the thicker 'cream' that rises to the surface. The liquid that remains is coconut milk.

Preparing Prawns

Prawns are an essential ingredient in Thai cooking, and Thai cooks always use uncooked king prawns in preference to the smaller variety.

To prepare fresh prawns, start by removing the heads – they should pull away fairly easily. Peel off the skins, working from head to tail, then remove the sharp, central rib of the tail, leaving the side pieces.

With a sharp knife, cut each prawn along the centre, stopping short of its tail. Open out and remove the central vein.

Preparing Squid

Prepare each squid by removing the head. Cut away and discard the eyes. With hands dipped in salt, rub the skin off the body, and remove the long internal quill-like bone, leaving each squid body intact. Use as required.

63

Index